COUNTERPOINT
THE POLYPHONIC VOCAL STYLE
OF THE SIXTEENTH CENTURY

KNUD JEPPESEN

Translated by Glen Haydon
With a new foreword by Alfred Mann

DOVER PUBLICATIONS, INC.
NEW YORK

IN GRATEFUL MEMORY OF
MY DISTINGUISHED TEACHER AND FRIEND
CARL NIELSEN

This Dover edition, first published in 1992, is an unabridged republication of the edition originally published by Prentice-Hall, Inc., New York, in 1939. (The original Danish edition was published by Wilhelm Hansen, Copenhagen, in 1931.) The foreword by Alfred Mann was specially written for the Dover edition. The errata of the original edition have been corrected directly in the text of the present edition.

Manufactured in the United States of America
Dover Publications, Inc., 31 East 2nd Street, Mineola, N.Y. 11501

Library of Congress Cataloging-in-Publication Data

Jeppesen, Knud, 1892–1974
    [Kontrapunkt (vokalpolyfoni). English]
    Counterpoint : the polyphonic vocal style of the sixteenth century / Knud Jeppesen ; translated by Glen Haydon ; with a new foreword by Alfred Mann.
        p.   cm.
    Translation of: Kontrapunkt (vokalpolyfoni).
    Translation originally published: New York : Prentice-Hall, 1939.
    ISBN 0-486-27036-X (pbk.)
    1. Counterpoint.   I. Title
MT55.J542   1992
782.2'21286—dc20

            91-40595
            CIP
            MN

FOREWORD

COUNTERPOINT, the title of Knud Jeppesen's textbook, issued in its original Danish edition in 1931, suggests at once in its terse formulation the unusual quality of this work. It is a quality one is tempted to describe with a word that, well worn today, seems nevertheless particularly apt in this case: authenticity. Jeppesen's *Counterpoint* stands apart from other manuals of the kind because the author considers its subject as a didactic phenomenon in its totality. He reviews its history in an opening chapter, and against this background he singles out the style of Palestrina as a pedagogical basis. But he does this with an authority unmatched by any of the authors who had taken a similar approach, because his textbook was preceded by a critical investigation of this style, a major scholarly achievement which was published under the title *The Style of Palestrina and the Dissonance* (original Danish edition 1923, English edition 1927). This monograph, in turn, was followed by more detailed studies, such as his essay dealing with a special aspect of the correlation between melodic and rhythmic accents as an idiomatic feature in Palestrina's music and its reflection in contrapuntal theory.[1]

The study of counterpoint had existed for about a thousand years, although, as Jeppesen explains, the term itself was not used in the earliest contrapuntal treatises. It emerged about 1300, and it is fascinating to see the work of Johannes Tinctoris, "the first great theorist in the modern sense" (p. 8), arise in Jeppesen's account against a background richly prepared. It is important, however, to realize that the word "theorist" itself is here not used in the modern sense because, unlike their latter-day confrères, the earlier authors of theoretical works were composers in their own right. Jeppesen's "Outline History of Contrapuntal Theory" is especially valuable because it links—both in his own writing and in that of the theorists he quotes—the names of the great masters, from Dufay to Bach, to the theoretical literature of their respective eras. In this survey he arrives at the significant point where contrapuntal theory was "in the

---

[1] "Das Sprunggesetz des Palestrinastils bei betonten Viertelnoten," in *Report on the International Musicological Congress*, Basel, 1925 (Leipzig: Breitkopf & Härtel).

process of changing from a discipline concerned with describing a style as best it can to one which emphasizes pedagogical ends" (p. 37).

The origin of this orientation is found in the generations of writers who raised the style of Palestrina to a didactic norm. It becomes clear from Jeppesen's text that this came about by a gradual process which indeed required the perspective of time. The foremost theorist among Palestrina's contemporaries, Gioseffo Zarlino, was still guided, as Jeppesen explains, by the model of Josquin rather than that of Palestrina. Yet his formulations proved to be so cogent that they were paraphrased in theoretical works for more than a century. We see in these books a curious mixture of adherence to the old rules and awareness of continually changing styles. The first to break away from this pattern was Johann Joseph Fux, Master of the Imperial Chapel in Vienna and one of the most eminent composers of his time.

Fux so consciously adopts the Palestrina style that he declares himself the student of Palestrina in the dialogue form of his text. It is Fux's historical as well as his pedagogical judgment that has rendered his book timeless. In very objective terms, Jeppesen states his own resulting indebtedness to Fux; in Jeppesen's work the student finds the traditional study of counterpoint enhanced and clarified by the exploration of its sources.

An inherent problem of Jeppesen's writing is its dualistic nature. Of necessity he speaks both as a historian and as a practitioner. The modern reader may be taken aback by the fact that, as early as in the Preface, Jeppesen quotes his own contrapuntal writing as a model, and that at the beginning of the actual instruction he adds the note, "The cantus firmi numbers 1, 6, and 20 are by Fux; the others by the author" (p. 107). A fine distinction may be observed here in that Fux referred in the choice of his cantus firmi expressly to chant. But Fux mixed melodies of Gregorian derivation with his own, and a key to this dichotomy is given in Jeppesen's statement that "the teacher or the pupil may, if he so chooses, compose for himself similar basic melodies" (p. 107). He logically concludes that it is "advisable to begin with the practice of writing pure one-voice melodies, since it cannot be too strongly emphasized that the linear idea dominates in counterpoint" (p. xv).

Here, too, he offers important fresh advice, and thus he proves his role as a historian of wide vision even where he seems to depart from it. The student is forever obliged to realize that an ultimate standard cannot be established; the "model" remains an ideal for which to strive. It is amusing to read in the writing of the twentieth-century composer Ernest

Bloch, himself a faithful disciple of Fux's system, that among the innu-
merable cantus firmi he wrote for purposes of study are some that are
"almost as bad" as the ones he found in the textbooks.

***

It was greatly to the credit of Glen Haydon, one of the outstanding
figures among American musicologists of the past generation, that he recognized the unique stature of Jeppesen's work and presented it in a first
English edition. He did this with great sensitivity to the text of the editions published under the author's own supervision, and he added some
valuable comments in the brief translator's introduction. The Dover re-
print of Haydon's translation in unchanged form is therefore to be
warmly welcomed.

Eastman School of Music   ALFRED MANN
University of Rochester
August 1991

INTRODUCTION
TO THE ENGLISH TRANSLATION

A s suggested by the title, Dr. Jeppesen's *Counterpoint* is a textbook on the polyphonic vocal style of the sixteenth century. But it is no ordinary textbook, because it maintains an unusually happy balance between theoretical and practical problems, between historical and systematic methodology. It is a practical manual designed for classroom use in teaching modal counterpoint, the logical successor of the old strict or academic counterpoint [1] and at the same time it affords invaluable material for the musicological seminar in which style-critical problems are under consideration. The present work is distinguished from the conventional treatise on counterpoint by its freedom from arbitrary rules and by its close adherence to a definite style period as a standard of reference. More and more, thoughtful musicians have come to realize that one cannot teach counterpoint "in general" without inviting endless controversy as to what is permissible and what is not. Hence a textbook based upon sound scholarly research in the music of a great period in the history of the art brings welcome relief to the serious but perplexed student and teacher of counterpoint.

The following suggestions may be helpful. Although the book is generously supplied with musical examples, students should be required to examine other works of the period for purposes of comparison and performance. I have found the *Laudate Pueri* [2] collection of sixteenth cen-

---

[1] See the translator's paper on "Music Research and Modal Counterpoint" in the *Yearbook* of the Music Educators' National Conference for 1934, pp. 217–222, in which this point is discussed at some length.

[2] *Laudate Pueri: Sacred Music of the XVIth Century . . . being the first part of the Northlands Singing Book,* selected and edited by Donald F. Tovey (London: Augener Ltd., 1910). Larger libraries have the complete editions of the works of Palestrina by Breitkopf und Härtel. The following editions are also recommended: Raph. Casimiri, *Societatis Polyphonicae Romanae,* 6 vols., and J. H. Rostagno & Giovanni d'Alessi, *Quinta Vocalis Liturgica* and *Anthologia Sexta Vocalis Liturgica,* Editione Marcello Capra, No. 201–202, and *Examples of Gregorian Chant and Works by Orlandus Lassus and Giovanni Palestrina,* compiled by Gustave Fredric Soderlund (Rochester, N. Y:. Eastman School of Music, University of Rochester, 1937).

tury vocal music, edited by Donald Francis Tovey, very helpful in this connection. Before beginning three-part writing, students should try their hands at writing two-part motets using the motets of Lassus as models. After the first exercises on imitation in two parts, I have students join two of these sections together. The chief problems in this work are the use of imitation, the treatment of the intermediate cadence so as to avoid too pronounced a rhythmical break, and the construction of a strong final cadence. From this sort of exercise to the construction of a motet of modest dimensions is but a step. Students are not only encouraged and pleased by such efforts but they derive great benefits therefrom. A verse or two from the Psalms or a simple couplet or quatrain will afford an ample text.

The course in modal counterpoint in the sixteenth century style is introduced in the third year of the curriculum in music at the University of North Carolina. Other institutions introduce it in the second or even the first year of the undergraduate course, while still others pursue such studies in the graduate school. And strangely enough I believe either one of these plans can be justified—on different grounds, of course. Opinions may vary as to the best time to introduce the study of counterpoint in the curriculum, but in my opinion the important point is not when it shall be introduced but rather, first of all, that it be introduced somewhere in the program and, second, that it be taught so as to give the student some insight into the principles of musical style both with respect to what is characteristic of the period and with respect to what is common to great musical compositions in many different periods.

GLEN HAYDON

Chapel Hill, North Carolina

PREFACE

MY BOOK on the style of Palestrina, in which I investigated certain polyphonic problems of the sixteenth century in detail,[1] was exclusively a historical study of style, although the conclusions necessarily have pedagogical importance because of the close relation of the subject to contrapuntal theory. In spite of the purely scientific character of the treatise, therefore, attempts have been made to use it as a textbook in counterpoint at some German universities, though probably with little success. I believe, however, I am justified in concluding that, at the present time, a need is felt for a textbook in counterpoint which takes into consideration the more recent research in the field of Palestrina's music. This thought has given me the desire and courage to work out this book.

I have therefore based my work on the laws of the Palestrina style, an idea which may seem strange to some. Of course I do not mean that modern composers should make Palestrina's style of expression their own —for that matter there seems to be little danger of this. Nevertheless I am convinced, just as a whole series of theorists have been for centuries, that from the style of Palestrina we can learn best what has always been the highest goal of the study of counterpoint.

It is recognized that musical theory has a retrospective as well as a descriptive character. Nobody has ever begun by manufacturing rules out of whole cloth. First came music itself; only later could the principles of its creation—its theory—be deduced.[2] Moreover it is well known,

---

[1] *The Style of Palestrina and the Dissonance*, Oxford University Press, 1927; the original German edition was published by Breitkopf und Härtel, Leipzig, 1925.

[2] The contrary—that theory preceded practice—may at certain points in the history of music seem more in agreement with the facts. For example, in the twelfth- and thirteenth-century art of the motet (the so-called *ars antiqua*), the "Franconian" law, setting forth a prohibition against dissonances upon accented portions of the measure, was formulated by the theorists some time before it was carried out in actual practice. Likewise, although the prohibition against parallel fifths was proclaimed in the thirteenth century and was made more stringent by the theorists of the

even among those only superficially acquainted with the music of various epochs, that no one style has ever had a command of all aspects of musical technique. Usually each historical period or school concentrates upon its own peculiar fundamental problems and more or less neglects the others. A musician who wishes to gain command of a particular technique must first decide just what it is he wishes to acquire, so that he can accordingly study those composers who mastered that technique. One wishing to acquire compact, forceful voice leading naturally would not go to Chopin; nor would one study Obrecht for a refined, sensitive use of chromatic harmony.

In counterpoint—the art of preserving the melodic independence of the voices in a polyphonic, harmonically balanced complex—only two periods are to be considered seriously: the culminations in polyphonic music characterized by the names of Palestrina and Bach. Here we have a choice, and here, too, the ways divide.

A series of theorists extending far back into the sixteenth century based their teaching upon Palestrina. Among them were Cerone, J. J. Fux, Cherubini, Albrechtsberger, S. W. Dehn, Heinrich Bellermann, Haller, Rockstro, Prout, Kitson, Morris, Stöhr, Schenker, and Roth. Another group, which began with John Philip Kirnberger and included E. F. Richter, S. Jadassohn, and Hugo Riemann, chose the art of Bach as its stylistic basis. Ernst Kurth, who has recently joined this group, gives a clear, concise definition of the term *counterpoint* in the following words: [3]

---

fourteenth, one cannot regard it as having been fully observed until the appearance of the *a cappella* composers of the Palestrina period. Both prohibitions, however, present only apparent exceptions—effects through whose operation theory and practice react upon one another. Theorists discover in practical music a particular tendency, at first only slightly developed, and translate their observations thereof into rules. But, according to their professional custom, they formulate these rules in an all too categorical and inelastic manner. Later, young composers who wish to gain practical knowledge study the writings of the theorists. A rule, once it is formulated on paper, can exert an influence out of all proportion to the importance previously attributed to it—can, indeed, exercise an almost magic power. It becomes dangerous. Out of respect for what is written down, composers strive, perhaps half consciously, to bring their practice into the nearest possible accord with the inscribed rules. And thus the influence of theory reacts upon practice. A similar chain of reactions is to be found in the history of the Nordic languages. In Denmark, for example, at the beginning of the past century, pronunciations were common that varied more widely from the older ones than do those of current Danish speech—a fact that might suggest a somewhat peculiar development curve. But here, too, the explanation is to be found in the influence that the written word exerts upon practice. At the beginning of the nineteenth century, in Denmark, there was an unusually great increase of skill in reading. Thus, the written language, which, in comparison to ordinary spoken language, is always rather unchanging and conservative, exercised an influence upon the latter, and caused it to revert to earlier pronunciations.

[3] Ernst Kurth: *Grundlagen des linearen Kontrapunkts.* Bern, Haupt, 1917. Page 143.

The essence of the theory of counterpoint is how two or more lines can unfold simultaneously in the most unrestrained melodic development, not by means of the chords but in spite of them.

Here Kurth is undeniably right; but from his hypothesis he finds the style of Palestrina less usable than Bach's as a basis for the teaching of counterpoint. He writes of the former: [4]

> The inner dissolution of the linear foundation is shown in the weakening of the melodic independence of the voices. Their melodic treatment is more and more determined by the harmonic element; the lines adjust themselves to the progression of the chordal structure; the play of free melodic invention is reduced to gentler, wave-like motions—to undulations more levelled in contour and range; and the melodic effects, especially of the middle parts, are absorbed by harmonic effects.

It cannot be denied that in the Palestrina style, especially in homophonic passages and cadences, melodic idioms occur that are clearly the result of harmonic considerations. These, however, are only exceptions. For that matter, similar passages occur in every kind of style—and not least in Bach's. On the other hand I have found that, in Palestrina's style, the vertical, harmonic requirements assume merely the exclusively consonant, full harmony of the chords, in which modulatory relations play only a small part. In Bach, however, certain chordal impulses, as Spitta has indicated, lie at the base of the musical structure; a certain modulatory disposition is present.

Bach's and Palestrina's points of departure are antipodal. Palestrina starts out from lines and arrives at chords; Bach's music grows out of an ideally harmonic background, against which the voices develop with a bold independence that is often breath-taking.

One should avoid comparisons between music and other arts; they are on the whole so different in character and material that a comparison is apt to prove quite pointless. Nevertheless, one parallel is so striking that I feel it is worth mentioning, a parallel juxtaposing, on the one hand, the mutual relations between the polyphonies of Bach and Palestrina and, on the other (in the field of art), the relations between the visual forms of expression of the renaissance and the baroque. In the sixteenth century there existed a polyphony that grew into a unified whole from single lines by virtue of the artistically controlled relation governing them; and

---

[4] *Ibid.*, p. 123.

in the field of the plastic arts there existed the art of the renaissance, swayed by a similar relation. With reference to this art, Heinrich Wölfflin has written in his *Kunstgeschichtliche Grundbegriffe*: [5]

> In this type of classical arrangement the separate parts assert an independence, regardless of how closely they may be bound up in the whole. The independence is not the aimless one of primitive art; each separate detail is conditioned by the whole without, however, ceasing to be an entity.

In baroque painting, for example in Rembrandt and Rubens, the unity is no longer a result; the artist begins with unity and works toward multiplicity. Certain broad principles of construction, such as that affecting the fall of the light, underlie the composition of the paintings. The details that lend interest or suspense grow out of the whole. Not for a moment is there a danger that the presence of too many details, standing strangely and coldly in opposition to one another, may prevent the observer from experiencing a sense of unity. This danger, we may suppose, assailed the beholder of the paintings of the early Middle Ages and the listener to the motets of the *ars antiqua*. The unity in baroque painting has pre-existence; it is the point of departure and the foundation of the whole. Again I should like to quote Wölfflin: [6]

> What, then, the baroque brings that is new is not unity in general, but that basic conception of absolute unity in which the part as an independent value is more or less submerged in the whole. No longer do beautiful individual parts unite in a harmony in which they continue to maintain their individuality; the parts have been subordinated to a dominant central motive, and only the combined effect of the whole gives them meaning and beauty.

What Wölfflin says of baroque painting may well be applied, in the field of music, to the art of Bach. For example, as the light permeates Rembrandt's "Night Watch," so a broad formative element is at the core of Bach's music. This element is a motivating impulse, a chordal-modulatory one. It is a streak of light which, to be sure, breaks up under the polyphonic approach, as if through a prism, into a glistening, sparkling play—a play whose variety, nevertheless, depends to a certain extent upon illusion.

Naturally, nothing has been said regarding the polyphonic values in

---

[5] Fourth Edition. Munich, Bruckmann, 1920. Page 16.
[6] *Ibid.*, p. 198.

Bach's art, or in Palestrina's; in both they are immeasurable. From the pedagogical viewpoint, however, the art that takes chords into consideration the least must doubtless afford the best starting point for acquiring the technique of independent voice leading.

Especially in Palestrina's favor in this connection seems to be the very strict economy of his style. It functions with such small, nicely calculated means, and it husbands its effects so carefully, that surely nowhere else can one better learn to know and understand polyphonic material in its most minute details. It may be said that in no other musical style does the fundamental contrast between consonance and dissonance appear so clearly as in Palestrina's. This is an advantage that can hardly be overestimated, especially in a period quite as prodigal with notes as ours.

*   *   *

Of all the tasks of music theory, among the most important is that of making us as vividly conscious as possible of what we are really trying to do, and of how countless are the possibilities inherent in even the simplest musical means. Musical theory may neither entirely disregard contemporary practice nor follow it blindly. It may even at times have the specific task of vigorously opposing recent tendencies, of exposing deficiencies of technique in contemporary composition, of pointing out the remedy, the path toward recovery. But it is nowhere prescribed that music theory must keep anxiously up to date. Its duty is only this: to endeavor to lead us to musical values, regardless of whether these are to be found in the present or the past.

Whoever wants to learn must first of all know what he wants to learn; but he must also realize that he cannot learn everything from any single source. In each of the great composers—whether Palestrina, Bach, Mozart, or one of the others—we find values that are most closely associated with the personality of the particular artist. Hugo Riemann is therefore in error in his criticism of Bellermann's *Kontrapunkt* (based upon Fux's *Gradus ad Parnassum,* which in turn is, as I have said, based on the style of Palestrina) when he asserts that Fux's work was already out of date at the time of its publication in 1725. Riemann naturally had to regard it so, because for him Bach polyphony was the only acceptable basis for all study of counterpoint, and to this type of polyphony the work of Fux could not lead, nor was it intended that it should. One cannot properly declare a textbook outmoded until another pedagogical work appears that performs the same tasks better, that is; produces the same musical values in fuller measure. But in 1725 the *Gradus* stood forth entirely unchallenged as the best counterpoint manual of its kind, and it justly maintained its reputation for a long time thereafter.

I do not mean that the *Gradus* is without its faults from a pedagogical viewpoint. On the contrary, I also believe that, even if Fux and the theorists who have shared his stand have chosen a favorable stylistic basis (indeed, for pedagogical purposes the *most favorable* stylistic basis), their position becomes decidedly vulnerable to criticism as soon as we ask whether they were able to make full use of the possibilities to which their right beginning should have led.

We find, for example, that Fux, who expressly declares in his *Gradus* that he has chosen Palestrina as his model, stands only in a somewhat remote relation to Palestrina's music. There are three reasons for this: Fux could have known comparatively few of Palestrina's works, for they were not commonly available in the eighteenth century; he was to a considerable degree dependent upon the older Italian theorists, who taught counterpoint more as "harmony" (it was not necessary to dwell especially upon the linear element because, at the time, such matters were taken for granted); and he involuntarily allowed the musical idioms of his own time to creep into his style.

What I say about Fux applies also, though perhaps to a lesser extent, to the writers of nearly all textbooks subsequently based upon him. The objection has justly been raised against them, as against Fux, that they promote a chordal rather than a linear style. Critics have especially deplored the fact that these theorists begin with exercises in "note against note." These critics say that whatever tendency the individual voices might have to attain melodic independence is completely paralyzed by such exercises, for with them it is a matter not of setting one line against another, but one single tone against another. It may be observed at this point that, even though the rhythmic identity of all the voices certainly does not help to give them melodic independence, yet a certain degree of independence may be attained through this type of drill. It can hardly be denied that a style such as that of the first example on page 112 (which, to be sure, does not come from Fux) is markedly linear. Each of the two added voices is characterized by a strong, compact linear construction and attains a melodic climax with undeviating sureness. The upper added voice reaches it at the beginning of the musical line, while the lower one reaches it only toward the end. In general I am firmly convinced that, if the polyphonic worth of the examples given as models by Fux and his followers is slight, the fault lies not with the system itself but rather with inadequate application of its latent powers. For in reality an almost entirely untapped mine of linear possibilities lies hidden here.

I therefore consider it unnecessary to abandon the system. I feel impelled to preserve what parts of it seem to me valuable—among other things, the "species" so frequently and energetically attacked. For, in spite of all apparent pedantry, they are based upon an idea that is sound and excellent. In the first place, they assure graded progress from the easiest to the most difficult, an advantage that Kirnberger especially praised as one of the most valuable features in the teaching of Bach. Further, they reveal the highly important relation of the tones to one another, their vigor or feebleness, the strength of the culmination notes, and their dependence upon the context. The basic idea of the system is indeed just this: that one must at first let the rhythmic problem be as simple as possible, in order to be able to concentrate the more intensively upon the purely melodic elements. Only when one has fully mastered these basic musical phenomena is the rhythm freed. Certainly it is pedagogically right to develop the melodic problem separately. But one would be wise to provide, in the study plan, a greater and more important place than has been customary for the stage at which melody and rhythm are free—the stage employing what Fux calls the fifth species, or florid counterpoint, to which the other species are merely preparatory.

Also, I consider it advisable to begin with the practice of writing pure one-voice melodies, since it cannot be too strongly emphasized that the linear idea dominates in counterpoint. Above all, the teacher as well as the pupil may well seek a much stricter command of the laws of the Palestrina style than can be found in Fux. This theorist, as I have said, was only moderately acquainted with the works of Palestrina. But today the large complete edition of Palestrina's works is available and musicological method is in general much more refined. It is perfectly natural that we should have far more accurate knowledge concerning Palestrina's style than was to be gleaned in the eighteenth and nineteenth centuries. Our advantages must be utilized. And, in conclusion, what has been implied in the foregoing may here be explicitly affirmed: a new work on counterpoint may claim distinction in relation to earlier textbooks, by virtue of its closer connection with Palestrina's style and its greater stress upon the linear element—a stress that logically follows.

KNUD JEPPESEN

CONTENTS

Part I
PRELIMINARIES

Part II
CONTRAPUNTAL EXERCISES

PART I

Preliminaries

Chapter I

OUTLINE HISTORY OF CONTRAPUNTAL THEORY

T HE WORD *counterpoint* presumably originated in the beginning of the fourteenth century and was derived from *punctus contra punctum,* "point against point" or "note against note."

COUNTERPOINT AND HARMONY CONTRASTED

When we use this expression today, we have a much more concrete, well-defined concept than was had formerly. In the Middle Ages and during a part of more modern times, counterpoint meant quite simply the same as polyphony. Today, however, we think of counterpoint as one particular style among other polyphonic types. Just as *polyphony* immediately suggests the contrasting idea, *homophony,* so the term *counterpoint* calls to mind the correlative concept, *harmony.* For us, music falls into two large divisions: polyphony, in which we perceive the chief structural elements in terms of melodic lines, that is to say, horizontally; and homophony, in which the fundamental consideration is the harmonic structure, or, as we may say, the vertical aspect of music.

These two styles or types of musical perception are distinguished particularly in the attitude towards chords. In harmony chords are presupposed: they are what is given and do not require any discussion; we submit ourselves to them and attempt to derive the laws for their treatment out of their reciprocal relations and inner states of tension. The situation is quite different in counterpoint: we begin not with chords but with melodic lines. Here chords are the result of several lines sounding simultaneously; hence they are product, not postulation. As always in matters of art, there arises a "not only . . . but also" relation: we must not only achieve *this, but* at the same time we must *also* give its due to a *something else,* which is hardly compatible.

The problem is not only to write beautiful and independent melodies in all parts, but also at the same time to develop the chordal combinations as fully as possible. We must write fresh, lifelike harmonic progressions and yet preserve a natural, convincing voice leading. Most highly cultivated polyphonic music will hold up under investigation from either the linear or the harmonic viewpoint. The best results of contrapuntal and of harmonic instruction are, therefore, in the last analysis, almost identical. Indeed in counterpoint and in harmony we strive for the same ideals and work through the same materials, but the approaches are from opposite directions. This difference in the point of departure, however, has such a telling effect upon practice that it seems appropriate to maintain two disciplines where ideally one might be sufficient. For practical pedagogical reasons it is worth while to keep the subjects separate. If, on the other hand, a more scientific explanation of the causes of musical effects and laws is desired, then one viewpoint should not be isolated from the other. If we wish to know, for example, why a particular treatment in a harmonization is elastic and lifelike, we seldom find the answer in harmony alone. Usually special contrapuntal factors, such as voice leading, must also be taken into consideration, just as we could not get very far in the opposite situation without considering harmony. Many mistakes and misleading explanations in counterpoint and more especially in harmony are due to failure to understand this simple fact.

As has already been said, the point of departure is of very real practical significance. It is by no means immaterial whether we say, as in contrapuntal teaching, "First the lines and then, in spite of them, the best possible harmonies"; or, as in the teaching of harmony, "First the chords and afterwards, so far as possible, good voice leading."

The Ninth to the Fourteenth Centuries: The Beginnings of Contrapuntal Theory

Let us return to the history of counterpoint. Originally, as we know, *counterpoint* meant polyphonic composition or composition in general. The first textbooks of counterpoint that are known to us, although they do not use this term at all, are based, therefore, on the oldest form of European polyphonic music of which examples are preserved for us, on the so-called parallel organum (about 900 A. D.). By "parallel organum" is meant the principle of musical construction by which a principal voice or part, generally a sacred "Gregorian" melody, is accompanied by one or more voices (by doublings in octaves) chiefly in parallel fourths or fifths.

This technique of composition is so little in accord with later concepts of musical law and procedure that in the beginning of the past century, when a serious interest in the history and evolution of music was very much in evidence, people were inclined to look upon the *Musica enchiriadis* and the other treatises of Hucbald, Guido, and the other earliest writers, as purely free speculations and theoretical fancies. It was asserted that such a form of musical composition never existed at all, and what is more, from a viewpoint characteristic of the nineteenth century, one even spoke of its "moral impossibility." In more recent times, however, especially through the investigations of comparative musicology, we have come to realize that song in parallel fourths and fifths is quite an ordinary phenomenon among peoples who, judged by our standards, are on a low musical plane. It is found, for example, among peoples of the Far East, among others in Burma, Siam, and China. Indeed it can still be heard in southern Europe, when people without musical training improvise in several parts. This oldest polyphonic theory, which plainly had some practical basis, is of course as primitive in character as the music upon which it is based. It has discovered that fourths and fifths sound good together, and it now exploits this discovery to the most extreme limits. Otherwise, however, it gives no further thought as to what might sound good together. Aside from the favorite intervals already mentioned, consonances and dissonances seem about equally good.

Hucbald

The treatise *Musica enchiriadis,* which was formerly attributed to Hucbald, contains a rule which prescribes certain restrictions with reference to the range of the free lower parts for the purpose of avoiding the dissonant fourth (*tritonus*). Remarkably enough, however, Hucbald himself does not even observe this rule logically. Besides, seconds, which are dissonances of much sharper character than those one was supposed to avoid, are introduced in the examples repeatedly. There is no reason why one should speak of any sort of dissonance treatment; the whole must be characterized as a very general preference for certain consonances on the one hand, and a not too logical avoidance of certain dissonant combinations on the other.

Contemporary music theory quite naturally reflects the evolution of polyphonic music in the course of the tenth and eleventh centuries. Parallel motion is gradually abandoned, partly to be replaced by the principle of consistent contrary motion (which is perhaps just as stiff and mechanical but musically much more fruitful) and partly to facilitate a freer treatment in general (which, as a matter of fact, was not unknown at an earlier date). Not until the music of the twelfth and thirteenth centuries, the so-called *ars antiqua,* do more stable rules for the treatment of the dissonance begin to develop and with them the rudiments of a real theory of counterpoint. Indeed, the theory of the treatment of the dissonance during this period shows that theorists gradually came to realize that there can be no talk of an art so long as melodic lines proceed with no regard for each other but ricochet along together without restraint in harsh, unclear tonal combinations. Here certain guarantees are required by the opposing viewpoint, by the vertical, the harmonic dimension. Only where tension exists between the two dimensions is polyphonic art in the deeper sense possible.

The Franconian Law

In the Franconian law, which seems to have come into being about the middle of the thirteenth century, we meet for the first time in the history of musical theory a genuine contrapuntal rule: "At the beginning of a measure in all modes (certain metrical orders), a consonance must be placed, regardless whether the first note is a long, a breve, or a semibreve." [1]

This law really pertains chiefly to rhythm, since it considers that so-called accented beats in the measure attract more attention, and are more prominent than the unaccented ones. It attains a validity which extends far beyond the time in which it was formulated. With a single

---

[1] *"In omnibus modis utendum est semper concordantiis in principio perfectionis licet sit longa, brevis vel semibrevis"* (Gerbert: *Scriptores ecclesiastici de musica sacra potissimum.* Typis San-Blasianis, 1784. Vol. III, p. 13). Indeed, this rule is to be found in somewhat more indefinite form in Johannes Garlandia's *"De Musica mensurabile positio"* (Coussemaker: *Scriptorum de musica medii aevi.* Paris, Durand, 1864. Vol. I, p. 107), whose treatise is considered somewhat older than that of Franco.

exception, the suspension dissonance, which is more apparent than real, it continues in force as long as the classical vocal polyphony prevails. Not until about 1600, when modern music begins, is its force broken. Even then it exercises a certain influence which is, to be sure, rather hidden.   One of the most important rules in the evolution of polyphonic music is thus comprehended by Franco and formulated for musical theory.

Another valuable advance in the endeavor to find a richer, more artistic style is the introduction of thirds and sixths, not merely as accidental harmonies, but as basic consonances, as factors upon which the musical structure primarily rests.   The technique of the *ars antiqua,* on the other hand, is based chiefly on the fifth.   If one examines a motet or any other polyphonic composition of the twelfth or thirteenth century, one finds fifths on most of the accented beats in the measure, combined for the most part with octaves.   Thirds and sixths occur more incidentally, generally on the unaccented parts of the measure.   They are thus used as dissonances, a circumstance that accords very well with the fact that throughout the greater part of the Middle Ages they were actually regarded as such and so classified.   In the meantime, there are many indications that in western Europe, especially in England and perhaps also in Scandinavia, thirds and sixths were used at a time when in other places—where the art was nevertheless perhaps more highly developed (as in France)—the fifth and octave were still used.   Statements of various medieval English theorists, it seems, as well as some contemporary musical works from the British Isles, must be understood in this sense.   At any rate, towards the end of the fourteenth and the ·beginning of the fifteenth century there is a whole series of important English composers who within a short time exercise an influence on the Continent, especially in the Netherlands and in France.   The most important thing in the art of these masters, that which means most for further development, is a new and fruitful attitude toward the consonance and thereby naturally also toward the dissonance.   While the position of the *ars antiqua* with respect to the matter of tonal combinations was rather indifferent and negative, and while about the only requirement was the demand for consonances on accented places (for the sake of transparency), this attitude seems from now on to take on a more positive form.   The chord becomes a factor which receives careful attention, and between the melodic and harmonic elements a certain tension arises, in which the melodic for the time being has the supremacy, which, however, it gradually relinquishes in the course of the fifteenth century, so that the state of balance between homophonic and polyphonic factors in the Palestrina style is made possible only after renewed inroads of the harmonic-vertical element (this time apparently through the popular music form of the beginning of the sixteenth century in Italy, the *frottola*).

The Fifteenth Century: Crystallization of Principles

In the course of the fifteenth century the polyphonic art develops and becomes established, and as early as the middle of the century one can speak of a music that is in the modern sense intellectually mastered, and in which the non-essential—the most dangerous, but not always equally well-known enemy of all art—is forcibly put on the defensive. Now arise the first great composers whose art is aesthetically satisfactory to us today without further reservations. Among them are Dunstable, Dufay, Binchois, Ockeghem, and Busnois and, in intimate relation with the practice of these musicians, the first great theorist in the modern sense, the Fleming, Johannes de Verwere, or Tinctoris, as his name is written in Latin.

Tinctoris

Tinctoris lived in Naples as Chapelmaster at the court of Ferdinand I. He wrote, among other things, a treatise called *De Contrapuncto* in the year 1477. This dissertation is in Latin, like most of the literature on musical theory of that time. The introduction, a well-known prefatory discourse addressed to King Ferdinand, reads somewhat as follows: [2]

Before I began to write, I strove to equip myself with the necessary knowledge of the various things pertaining to music, partly through listening to others and partly by my own reading and incessant work. However I do not write to bring honor to myself, but for the benefit of others who wish to study music, and further in order not to bury the talent which God has bestowed upon me. And therefore I have now undertaken to write briefly about counterpoint—which is made up of well-sounding consonances—in God's honor and for the use of those who are striving for skill in this excellent art. Before I proceed now with the work, I will not hide the fact that I have studied what the ancient philosophers, such as

[2] For this and the following quotations from the writings of Tinctoris, see Joannis Tinctoris *Tractatus de musica*, edited by E. de Coussemaker, Lille, 1875.

Plato and Pythagoras, as well as their successors, Cicero, Macrobius, Boethius, and Isidor, believe concerning the harmony of the spheres. Since, however, I have found that they differ very much from each other in their teachings, I have turned from them to Aristotle and to the more modern philosophers, and no one shall make me believe that musical consonances arise through movements of the heavenly bodies, for they can only be produced by means of terrestrial instruments. The ancient musicians, Plato, Pythagoras, Nichomachus, Aristoxenus, Archytas, Ptolemaeus, and many others, indeed even including Boethius himself, dealt extensively with the consonances, and yet we do not know at all how they arranged and classified them. And if I must now refer to that which I have seen and learned, I must confess that some old compositions of unknown composers have come into my hands, pieces that sound quite simple and tasteless, so that they rather disturb than please the ear. However, what surprises me especially is that only in the last forty years are there compositions which, in the judgment of the specialist, are worth listening to. Today, however, we have blossoming forth, quite apart from the large number of famous singers—whether it be on account of heavenly influences or particularly zealous studies—an almost unlimited number of composers, for example Johannes Ockeghem, Johannes Regis, Antonius Busnois, Firminus Caron, Guilelmus Faugues, and all can boast of having had as teachers the musicians who died recently, Johannes Dunstable, Egidius Binchois and Guilelmus Dufay. Nearly all the works of these masters excel in pleasant sound; I never hear or look at their compositions without rejoicing in them or being instructed by them, and therefore I too, in my own compositions, adhere entirely to the approved style.

It is evident that Tinctoris was a practical musician who displayed an independence (quite foreign to his time) of the classic "auctores," otherwise regarded as unshaken authorities, and of their philosophical speculations. He turned directly to the musical works. He had a remarkable understanding of the decided break between the music of his time and that which immediately preceded it.

Tinctoris thereupon introduces his actual textbook, according to the custom of the time, with a definition of the subject:

Counterpoint is an artistic tonal combination which arises when one tone is placed opposite another, from which also the term *contrapunctus*, that is, note against note, can be derived. Counterpoint is therefore a combination of tones. If this combination or mixture sounds pleasant, it is called consonance; if, on the other hand, it sounds harsh and unpleasant, it is called dissonance.

Here Tinctoris gives no more comprehensive definition of counterpoint. What he says, however, is interesting. For example, he speaks exclusively of chords, and he derives the word *counterpoint* quite rightly from something purely vertical. On proper voice leading or melodic considerations, he wastes no words. As we already know, this omission is easy to understand, for the linear was for that period something taken for granted, that required no further explanation, while the secondary consideration, the harmonic, was more in danger of being neglected and therefore demanded especial attention and emphasis. This then is how it happens that a more prominent place is given to the harmonic element in the theoretical exposition, which, however, did not actually correspond to the practice.

Following this definition, Tinctoris observes that he wishes first to speak of the consonances, since they play the most important rôle in counterpoint, whereas dissonances are admitted only here and there. He then classifies the consonances in different ways, among others into perfect and imperfect consonances. In the first class he counts the unison, fourth, fifth, and octave, which, as he says himself, stand out in every composition and are the mainstay thereof. The imperfect consonances, in which he includes major and minor thirds and sixths, he considers less good. On this point he is remarkably conservative and dependent on earlier theorists. Concerning the minor sixth, which the older authors classed with the dissonances, he says, "In my ear, too, it sounds somewhat rough when it stands alone," and he therefore prefers that it be excluded from the two-part composition where it is most noticeable. Tinctoris then brings in a survey of the twenty-two consonances which he considers usable and finally presents the different possibilities of combinations and progressions. He shows, for example, how one can progress from a unison to a third, fifth, sixth, or octave, and how one proceeds from a third to another consonant interval. This discussion may seem somewhat pedantic and detailed to us, and yet we must consider how new the richer and more varied use of the consonances was at that time. It was by no means pointless to indicate all the possibilities that existed—possibilities that were certainly surprising to many.

In the second book of Tinctoris is the list of dissonances, which are tersely defined as combinations that sound bad. Among these Tinctoris places the minor and major second, the augmented fourth, the minor and major ninth, and so on. The perfect fourth he does not consider here, but remarks elsewhere that although the ancients considered it a consonance, it sounds so bad to the ears of trained musicians that it really can be used only if it occurs over a fifth, and so does not make a fourth in relation to the lowest voice but only to the middle part.

We might now expect Tinctoris to explain clearly, as he did with the consonances, how dissonances can be used with consonances and what combinations are available. But he does not discuss this point at all—apparently because he finds dissonances so unessential that such a careful presentation would be superfluous at this point. At any rate, he passes it over and goes on to the actual discussion of counterpoint.

He divides counterpoint into two types: *contrapunctus simplex,* in which notes of equal value are placed against each other, and *contrapunctus diminutus* or *floridus,* in which two or more notes of lesser value are placed against a note of greater value. Both kinds of counterpoint can be performed either from the notes (therefore previously composed) or extemporaneously. In the first case it is referred to as *res facta;* in the second, the manner of performing is called *super librum cantare* (to sing over the book). A counterpoint can be constructed either over a cantus firmus in notes of equal length, which is called *cantus planus,* or over a *cantus figuratus,* a melody consisting of notes of mixed time values. In "simple" counterpoint ("note against note") no dissonances are permitted at all. In counterpoint with more rhythmic movement, they may be used under certain conditions. Tinctoris says in this regard that more dissonances than consonances occur in the compositions of his predecessors, but he observes further that in improvised counterpoint, dissonances actually occur only in short note values and on unaccented beats, or as suspensions. Dissonances must always be treated in stepwise progressions; a skip of a third is rarely permissible. Tinctoris further considers it bad to return after a dissonance to the preceding consonance. In other words, he forbids auxiliary notes even if they occur in very short note values, and he thereby formulates a rule which is not entirely in accord with the practice, but nevertheless which serves him as a point of departure. There is also a discussion of the question concerning the length of note which may be used as a dissonance, and here Tinctoris' chief rule is that the longest note which may be dissonant is, in fact, a note equal in length to one-half the unit of measure. But he also cites examples showing that contemporary composers, Petrus de Domarto and Antonius Busnois for example, break this rule and write dissonances equal in length to the whole unit of measure.

In the third and last part of the work, eight principal rules of counterpoint are finally stated, of which the content is substantially as follows:

First rule: One must begin and end with a perfect consonance. If one begins with a rest (upbeat), then the entrance may be made with an imperfect consonance as well. It is also not wrong for singers who are improvising a counterpoint to close with an imperfect consonance. In such a case, however, the composition must be for several voices and the sixth (or its octave) above the bass must not be used.

Second rule: One must not accompany the tenor with perfect consonances of the same size, but one may very well do so with imperfect consonances. Some permit the direct succession of perfect consonances in the upper voices even when these consonances are the same size, and they allow such parallels if they are separated by a rest. Such a way of composing, however, is good only if a particularly beautiful effect is attained by it, or if it is required by strict imitation. This rule says, in other words, that parallel fifths and octaves are not permitted, whereas parallel thirds and sixths may very well be used.

Third rule: If the tenor continues on one and the same tone, both perfect and imperfect consonances may be added. Tones may also be repeated in the added contrapuntal part. Whenever the counterpoint is over a cantus firmus in notes of equal value, such repetitions of tones are not especially good. In *res facta,* that is, in written counterpoint, tonal repetition may well be used where the text warrants it.

Fourth rule: The counterpoint must continue in good melodic form even if the tenor makes large skips.

Fifth rule: A cadence is not permitted over any tone, whether high or low, if it interferes with the development of the melody.

Sixth rule: Redicta, that is, repetition of the same melodic idiom, is not permitted over a cantus firmus in notes of equal value, and least of all if the cantus firmus itself contains such a repetition. This applies likewise to written compositions, although one uses such idioms occasionally in order to imitate the sound of bells or of horns.

Seventh rule: Over a cantus firmus in notes of equal length, one should not allow two cadences on the same tone to follow one another too closely. Only as a last resort, therefore, should composers choose cantus firmi which invite melodic idioms like the *redicta.*

Eighth rule: One should always earnestly strive in contrapuntal writing for variety and change, by altering the measure or time, using now syncopations, now imitations, and the like. Yet one must keep in mind that a simple song does not use so many different means as a motet; and a motet likewise not so many as a mass.

By and large, we must look upon Tinctoris' contrapuntal method as a brilliant accomplishment for its time, the result of his own free reflection. Here speaks a musician who stands on the pinnacle of the musical technique of his time, who always understands its essential, central facts in their full significance. Behind his terse, matter-of-fact words, we can always recognize the artist, the practical musician whose speech is pleasingly free from the circumlocutious or confused phraseology of most of the theoretical works on music of his day. That Tinctoris deals almost exclusively with chords and harmonic problems in his discussion is undoubtedly due, as we have seen, to the whole attitude and disposition of the fifteenth century. Naturally, it would be fatal if this method of presentation were retained and applied to a later time in which the linear idea no longer was held basic. It is always dangerous to dwell unduly on a secondary consideration, for one thereby easily forgets the main point. One cannot help noticing this fault in a large part of the contrapuntal literature based upon Tinctoris which uncritically takes over his teaching.

THE SIXTEENTH CENTURY: THE STYLE OF PALESTRINA

With the sixteenth century arose the golden age of vocal polyphony. This art form, which had been most zealously cultivated during the preceding centuries by the English, French, and Netherlanders, was transplanted to Italy. With the way prepared by great masters, especially Josquin des Prez, it reached its consummation there, in the Roman school, in Palestrina and his pupils, and in masters of other nations (such as the Spaniards, Morales and Victoria, or the Netherlander, Orlandus Lassus), who had studied in Italy, where during the following centuries the most significant musical developments took place.

If the art of this period of florescence between 1560 and 1590 is compared with the music of the last part of the fifteenth century, significant differences will be seen. The differences in form are the least evident. In both periods are found approximately the same forms: the great artistic masses, in which the composers were able to reveal all aspects of their remarkable technique; the motets intended for church and chamber music, in which the art of fine detail was practiced; and finally the secular songs, chansons, Italian *frottole* and madrigals, as well as German *Lieder*. In the secular songs technical refinement often suffered because of the demands of popular taste, but experiments flourished. Here for the first time are found most of the elements which were new in the music of that time and which were to be the significant means of further development.

The essential difference between these two stages of development within the same movement lay, therefore, rather in content than in form. If the harmony of the fifteenth century was often a little ascetic and thin (we still find definite traces of the fifth and octave supremacy of the preceding century) nevertheless the compositions of the period when vocal polyphony flourished were distinguished by perfection in wealth and variety of tonal combinations. Empty fifths and octaves at least are very much suppressed and are not chosen for the sake of the sound; but when they do occur, they are always motivated by the movements of the melody, by voice leading, imitation, or the like.

Imitation (a principle in accordance with which the voices imitate each other by introducing the same theme in one voice after the other) was employed less fruitfully and logically at the end of the fifteenth century, but began to play a principal role in musical construction during the sixteenth century. In the first half of the sixteenth century, imitation was used at times with almost pedantic stiffness, which, however, seems to have brought about a natural and beneficial reaction in the works of Palestrina and other composers of the late sixteenth century.

Treatment of the Dissonance

The attitude toward the dissonance must be mentioned at this point.

During the earlier years, as we already know, dissonances themselves played no rôle, but were regarded as bad-sounding and unclear and were therefore kept off the accented parts of the measure as much as possible— without, however, being subjected to any particular rules. In the course of the fifteenth century the law for the conjunct treatment of dissonances became established, as has been pointed out, not only to a certain extent in actual practice but also in theory, especially as formulated by Tinctoris. Tinctoris suggested, however, the possibility that occasionally dissonances might be quitted by a skip of a third descending. If we investigate the practice of the great composers of the fifteenth century—Dufay, Binchois, Ockeghem, and Busnois for example (and even Josquin des Prez, who really belongs to the early sixteenth century), we see that this rule is not merely one devised by Tinctoris, but one well-rooted in the practice of the time.   During the sixteenth century the rule concerning the step-wise treatment of the dissonance became stricter.   Instances occur less often in which dissonances were introduced or quitted by skips of a third or the like, and in the Palestrina style this rule was strictly followed with only one apparent exception: the *cambiata.*

While the thirteenth and fourteenth centuries (the *ars antiqua* and the greater part of the *ars nova* period) only took this purely negative atti-tude toward the dissonance, by the fifteenth century the situation began to change.   The syncope dissonance, or suspension, gradually came to be used so frequently and under such circumstances that it was clearly used consciously for its effect.   In theory it is mentioned, apparently for the first time, by Guilelmus Monachus, a monk, whose treatise *De Praeceptis artis musice et practice compendiosus libellus* [3] contains much original and unique material.

Guilelmus introduces the treatise with a survey of the various note values and the complicated proportions and meters of that time.   He goes on to speak of the method of composition of the English, the faux-bourdon (in modern terms, a style of writing in parallel chords of the sixth).   Then follows a chapter on counterpoint as practiced by the English and French, in which he first surveys the different consonances (thirds and sixths belong to the imperfect consonances) and finally nine contrapuntal rules.   Of these rules, only the next to the last is of espe-cial interest here:

Although we have enumerated only twelve consonances (both perfect and im-perfect) nothing prevents us, according to the custom and practice of recent times, from using dissonances, as for example the second, which adds sweetness to the low third; or the seventh, which lends sweetness to the sixth; the fourth, which does likewise to the upper third; and this last again, which, according to recent experience, lends sweetness to the fifth.

Thus far Guilelmus.   He says nothing to the effect that he is referring to the syncope dissonance, the suspension; but there can be no doubt

---

[3] Coussemaker, *Scriptorum,* Vol. III, p. 291.

that he is speaking of it. The examples contained in the treatise show that Guilelmus was familiar with precisely this form of dissonance treatment; and the rules which he gives accord exactly with the laws observed in practice. It is obvious that he understands the matter thoroughly. When the rule says that the second is to be resolved in the low third (a somewhat vague way of saying that the dissonance must lie in the lower voice), and when it further provides that the seventh should be resolved in the sixth and the fourth in the "high" third (in the latter case the dissonance must therefore be introduced in the upper voice), obviously the very best and most common forms of resolutions of the suspension dissonance are intended, as the practice of the fifteenth and sixteenth centuries shows. If this passage applied to the passing dissonances, such a comprehensive exposition of the intervals of resolution would have been superfluous; for the passing second resolves just as well into the unison as into the third, the fourth as well into the fifth as into the third, and so on, according to whether the movement is ascending or descending.

Of great psychological significance is the expression which Guilelmus uses in expounding the use of the syncope dissonances, in that he speaks of the "sweetness" which they lend to the succeeding consonance. This indicates that the men of that time heard the syncope dissonance just as we hear it today, as a conscious introduction of dissonance in aesthetically stressed contrast to consonance—therefore not as something to be avoided or softened as much as possible, but as an effect which is in itself of great value and which cannot be replaced by any other effect. Zarlino, the great theorist of the sixteenth century, expressed himself in exactly this manner regarding the suspension dissonance:

Not only is such a dissonance not displeasing but, on the contrary, it arouses great pleasure through the increased mildness and sweetness which it lends to the succeeding consonance. And this for the reason that everything comes out much more clearly as soon as it is placed in contrast with its opposite.

This is the view of the fifteenth and sixteenth centuries; and what is more important than its specific consequence, the suspension, this conception influenced further development. It marks a great step in advance as compared with the crude, rather one-sided attitude of earlier times toward these matters.

The sixteenth century developed another feature in the use of the dissonance, a feature which, as a matter of fact, was not exploited fully until the following century: namely, *the dissonance as a means of poetical expression,* as a symbol of the emotions. This involves a factor in the process of evolution which influenced the history of music more, perhaps, than any other.

The Origin of the Style

Repeated attempts have been made to explain the origin of the style of Palestrina. Best known is the hypothesis of Hugo Riemann, which concludes from the assumption that most of the music of the fifteenth century was intended for instruments, that the evolution took place when people gradually went over to vocal performance of compositions, and various so-called "instrumentalisms" (idioms which Riemann conceives as having been designed especially for instruments) proved impractical because they were not suited to the nature of the human voice; and that the greater importance the singing voice attained in the process of evolution, the more the instrumental idioms were suppressed until they finally disappeared entirely. It is possible but by no means certain that Riemann is right when he assumes that a part of the music of the fifteenth century is instrumental music. At any rate it is most doubtful whether at that time musicians distinguished carefully between vocal and instrumental composition. Today it is difficult to imagine music without such a distinction; we run the danger, however, of anachronistic thinking if we apply our way of feeling, highly developed in this respect, to a period which apparently had not developed it.

It seems much more likely that the *attitude toward the text* may have been the impelling force in the rise of the Palestrina style.

While the treatment of the text in the fifteenth century was characterized for the most part by a striking indifference, and while the use of effective, unequivocal tone painting as a means of expression can be found only in very rare cases in European music before 1500, the sixteenth century brought a decisive change in this situation. The tendency came, apparently, chiefly from the madrigal (doubtless prepared by the *frottola,* however), the chief form of the Italian secular music of the sixteenth century. In general, secular music took the lead in the development, for religious music was almost always characterized by a certain conservative attitude.   In the beginning of the sixteenth century the *frottola* was flourishing in Italy.   This was a polyphonic composition in a very short and concise form, with but few imitations.   It was chordal, homophonic, and simple throughout.   It was used almost exclusively by Italian composers, but corresponding forms are to be observed among contemporary Spaniards.   As, however, the Netherlandian composers overran Italy at the beginning of the century and began to occupy themselves seriously with the *frottola,* a change in its character is observable; it maintained in part its original, vertical, chordal form, but was worked out in a richer and more refined musical manner, at times with imitation and other contrapuntal devices.   Also a gradual change took place in the text.   Though in the beginning it was for the most part naïvely cheerful, it became little by little an art of the court, a matter of polished, affected rhymes with a predilection for bombastic, exaggeratedly passionate ways of speaking.   The relation between word and tone is not very intimate in the *frottola* in spite of obvious attempts at rapprochement. In the madrigal, the more refined descendant of the *frottola,* expressive tendencies come ever more distinctly to the fore and a marked incongruity is felt between the robust, emotional text and the music, which is anything but overwrought, being excellent but remarkably abstract.   Likewise the fanatically humanistic attitude of the time, which placed the study of the ancient writers and music theorists so prominently in the foreground, had a pronounced influence upon the evolution of an expressive musical treatment of the text.   People now heard of the wonderful influence which the music of the ancients exercised upon their spirits, and among scholars the slogan arose, *"Dare spirito vivo alle parole* (give words living spirit by means of tones)."   They began to strive in all conceivable ways to construct the madrigal in the light of this saying, but the results in the beginning were strange and rather superficial. When, for example, poems mentioned an ascent or descent, the composer conscientiously attempted in the music the corresponding movements in the scale.   Musicians did not as yet have sufficient command of the necessary musical means of expression, but they tried persistently, and at any rate learned one thing: a deep respect for the text.   From now on it was unthinkable that the placing of the text should simply be left to the singer.   Everything essential was carefully prescribed, and the music was so composed that the text, unrestrained, came fully into its own.

Pope Marcellus II's famous admonition, which was sent to the papal singers on Good Friday in 1555 and which ordered the selection of a choral work suited to the sad character of this holiday, as well as the most careful attention to clear enunciation of the text, together with the re-formatory attempts of the Tridentine Council which were founded upon similar views, constitute interesting expressions of the general will to make music subordinate to the text. This tendency is transferred to sacred music from the madrigal, where it first begins to be noticeable, and in sacred music finds expression—at least with more conservative masters, such as Palestrina—chiefly in refined declamation and great respect for the text. Yet, besides the *frottola* and the madrigal, the secular *laude,* which flourished in Italy at the same time as the *frottola,* directly influenced the later development of sacred music.

The inclination toward the dramatic and programmatic is less pro-nounced, but it continues to be present. It constantly seeks for new ways and means of expression until finally, toward the end of the century, it forces its way through and creates in the opera the central form from which practically all modern music comes. The decisive change, how-ever, did not take place in the year 1594 or 1600, but at the moment when the concept appeared that music is not merely a decorative factor but a means of portraying human ideas and emotions. This new point of view marks the sharp distinction between the older and the newer music; the attitude toward the text is decisive in the evolution. And this attitude characterizes especially the music of the later sixteenth century in com-parison with that of a century earlier. It accompanied the general re-finement of musical technique and the superior culture. Melodies much more definitely tonal in character and treated with disproportionately greater architectonic mastery, greater fullness of the chords, and stricter use of the dissonance are here especially remarkable. From our present viewpoint we must characterize the music of Palestrina in this manner. Let us learn something of the judgment of its contemporary theorists.

Vicentino

Vicentino's famous work *L'Antica musica ridotta alla moderna prat-tica,* published in 1555, states excellently the typical contrapuntal theory of the sixteenth century. Even the title, "The Music of Antiquity Reduced for Modern Practice," is characteristic. Don Nicola Vicentino, a priest from Vicenza and a pupil of Adrian Willaert, the famous Netherland chapelmaster at St. Mark's church in Venice, was a zealous advocate of everything which he considered ancient music.   In 1546 he published a collection of "chromatic" madrigals, as he called them, and in the theoretical work just mentioned he demonstrated, according to the ancient models, not only the diatonic but also the chromatic and enharmonic tonal systems.   Detailed discussion of this expansive work, to a great extent decidedly experimental in character and devoted only slightly to the practice of the sixteenth century, would lead us too far afield.   Nevertheless various portions, especially those dealing with diatonic music, deserve consideration.   Vicentino emphasizes, for example, that in the composition of madrigals, among other things, little depends upon the pedantic maintenance of the mode and the like; most important is to see that life and breath be given the text by the tones and that the music express the passions and feelings, bitter as well as mild, cheerful as well as melancholy.   Elsewhere in his book he defends the use in suspensions of the augmented fourth, which is otherwise generally in disfavor, for expressing something rough or unpleasant.   The same line of thought can also be observed in the works of Zarlino and other famous theorists of that time, though one looks for it in vain in theoretical works of the preceding century.   It is a truly typical trait of the sixteenth century.

Otherwise Vicentino, apart from somewhat misguided efforts to introduce the use of chromaticism and enharmonics, contributes much that is valuable and new.   Because he mixes long-known facts and new observations in a confused and unorganized manner, his book makes a somewhat unfavorable impression; but it contains sufficient that is ingenious and significant to reveal Vicentino as an intuitive theorist and keen judge not only of contemporary music but also of the art of the past. Especially remarkable is his feeling for history, which was decidedly rare at that time when men almost never showed any interest in the genetic viewpoint.   In his discussions of the passing dissonances or *"dissonanze sciolte"* (free dissonances), this feeling is very noticeable.   For example, he says:

The reader will realize that in music, from time to time, some progress is made; in old-fashioned compositions we can see that the composers placed passing dissonances in whole notes against a breve (which is equal to two whole notes) whereby they let the first be a consonance on the strong beat while the second was a dissonance.

Later they felt these dissonances to be too tedious and abandoned this manner of composition; in order to disturb the ear less, they used half notes, the first being consonant on the strong beat, the second forming a dissonance on the weak beat, and this practice was continued for some time. Today this custom is no longer common because the half note as a dissonance is too prominent, and not only it but the quarter note as well is too sharp a dissonance if it is not used in a proper manner; we therefore are accustomed to use only quarters and eighths as dissonances.

Vicentino here gives us entirely trustworthy historical conclusions, except that he is mistaken when he says that dissonant half notes are completely excluded from the music of his time. It is true, however, that they occurred somewhat less frequently then than in earlier times and that quarter notes appeared more frequently as dissonances.

Vicentino also makes some pertinent and precise comments concerning quarters. He speaks of three syncope forms: major, if the syncopation is a breve; minor, if it has the value of a whole note; and minima, if it has the duration of a half note. All syncopation dissonances should be resolved by the downward progression of the second, and where possible an imperfect consonance should follow them because, as Vicentino writes, nature is not fond of extremes but prefers the middle way; a perfect consonance would make too sharp a contrast with the preceding dissonance. In addition, Vicentino sets up the reasonable rule that the resolving tone should have half the worth of the syncopation itself. One can also use syncopations without dissonance as long as syncopations do not occur simultaneously in all parts; if they should, one would not be able to get a clear impression of the syncopation at all.

After accented half notes, whether syncopated or not, the first of two quarters descending stepwise can be a dissonance, but only in descending motion; in the opposite direction only the second, unaccented, quarter may be made a dissonance. That Vicentino is a true son of the sixteenth century is seen especially in the chapter in which he gives definite rules concerning the placing of the text under the notes—such a matter would scarcely have interested a theorist of an earlier date. His detailed treatment of imitation is also a typical trait of the century; here we are told, among other things, that in imitation one should keep the voices in an easily understandable relation to each other and that imitations at the second, seventh, or ninth should be avoided so far as possible. Further, one should not delay the entrance of the theme in the accompanying voices too much, especially with four beats to a breve. That a theme which begins on a strong beat may be brought in on a weak beat in the imitation, provides for a valuable variation which will please the listener. One should avoid bringing in the soprano too high; doing so easily produces a harsh and unrefined effect. Vicentino further warns against beginnings with runs; rapid movements should grow out of slower ones. And apparently Vicentino is the first to introduce the rule concerning the tonal answer of the fugue theme: that a skip of the fourth must be answered by a skip of the fifth in order to preserve the unity of the key. He also speaks of double counterpoint, compositions for several choruses, and other problems belonging to a later time.

Vicentino therefore makes many significant observations; for the most part, however, he has not progressed a step beyond the theorists of the preceding century. Times have changed and with them style. Therefore the music which Vicentino discusses is different from that with which Tinctoris dealt. Both, however, had only vague notions of the real problems of counterpoint, simply because for those times, which received the polyphonic style as a gift at birth, so to speak, such problems scarcely existed.

But Vicentino is representative of only a certain aspect of the sixteenth century, of the "modern" in terms of what would be regarded modern in that time; to regard him as typical of the whole sixteenth century would be wrong, for he is too much of an individualist. With amazing shrewdness and astonishing boldness he discovered for himself the direction evolution was taking and gave frank expression to his views. He is typical of his age insofar as he expressed himself regarding some of the questions which most concerned the men of his time and for the solution of which they were most eagerly striving, although with little success. Although the sixteenth century quite unmistakably prepared the way for the seventeenth and with it for the rise of emotional, subjectively tinged music, it is clear that this characteristic is manifested more in its attempts than in its deeds. The real accomplishments of the sixteenth century are depicted by other theorists better and, above all, more temperately than by Vicentino. It must be considered, too, that the tendency to the expressive and subjective, which was predominant in the century and which characterizes this period in comparison with the preceding epoch, was cut across by somewhat strong counter-tendencies toward the objective and universal.

La Musica Comuna

The sixteenth century shows a certain preference for an aesthetic concept, *"la musica comuna,"* a phrase which is not easy to translate but which means something like easily comprehensible, regular, perhaps academic music. The sixteenth century loves clearness, directness, naturalness. It wants order, strict conformity to rule, and not too much of the superfluous. A more implacable critique than that of the sixteenth century has never been applied to the fantastic, ceremonious Gothic of the Middle Ages. For originality which is highly suggestive of genius, according to modern ideas influenced by romanticism, the sixteenth century had little understanding. The ideal of the composers was to work out their art in such a way that as many as possible could understand it and rejoice in it.[4]

No wonder Palestrina came as the greatest representative of an epoch which cherished these views. Posterity has rightly called him "the great imitator of nature" and indeed a gifted naturalness is expressed in all his works, a sure feeling for the occasional, the easily comprehensible, in short, for classical expression. His art seeks universality and is characterized by a deep joy in the development and fulfillment of the law. It is only slightly concerned with the new; the old is eternally new to it. Its essence is in depth; experimental expansion of the means of artistic expression is foreign to it. It is the perfect, masterly expression of the *musica comuna,* that movement within the music of the sixteenth century which dedicated itself to the past, but which in its way is so much more important and typical in the art of music of the time than the more forward-looking expressive tendency, *"la musica reservata"* (as the

---

[4] Indicative of this view is a letter which a certain Gian, an agent of the Duke Ercole Este of Ferrara, wrote at the beginning of the sixteenth century. He reports here the following concerning two of the greatest composers of the century, namely Josquin des Prez and Heinrich Isaac:

"I call your Highness' attention to the fact that the singer Isaac has been in Ferrara and has composed a motet on the theme 'La mi la sol la si la mi' which is very good and which he finished in two days. From this one cannot conclude otherwise than that he works very fast; besides this, he also composes in such a way that it pleases the people. . . . I find that he is better suited to serve your majesty than Josquin, because he has a more sociable manner and writes more that is new. It is true, however, that Josquin composes better; he acts, however, according to his own desire and pleasure and not according to the wishes of the people."

According to our present standard Josquin is more of a genius than Isaac. Even so, it is certain that Isaac, according to the letter, much more nearly met the demands which people of the sixteenth century made of a genius.

Netherlander Coclicus called the latter about the middle of the century).

To understand how this *musica comuna*—the Palestrina style, the generally used style of composition of the time—was formulated by the theorists, we will have to consider a confusing number of statements, several of which are quite convincing. When we observe, however, the number of rules which were set up in comparison with the number which might have been made, we are surprised to find that the former are extremely few. The greater the interval between the theorist and the time of which he writes, the easier he finds it to formulate a theory. It is much more difficult to see events near at hand in perspective than to see them from a little distance.

The result of the musical lawmaking of the sixteenth century is, however, not only quantitatively slight, but even important rules which every contrapuntist observed often either were not known at all by the theorists, or they are not mentioned—a remarkable circumstance which suggests that composers and theorists, perhaps for business reasons, only partially disclosed their knowledge.[5]

It is also possible that a remark of the German theorist Ottmar Luscinius (1487–1537)—that theorists of earlier times spoke so little about everything pertaining to the dissonance only because they regarded this theme as pertaining rather to practice than to theory—can be extended to apply to musical technique in general, so that we can assume that the teachers initiated their pupils into various "secrets" which they for various reasons did not see fit to write down or to publish.

It is well known that several of the great composers of the sixteenth century engaged in teaching. That Palestrina was a kind of conservatory director in Rome is, to be sure, only a legend; however, it has been proved that several of the important masters of the generation immediately following him were instructed and trained by him. So far as we know, however, he did not leave any written documents which might enlighten us as to the nature of his instruction. The only bit of writing which comes to our aid in this respect is a letter which he, as a famous master, wrote to the Duke of Mantua, Guilelmo Gonzaga. This prince was a

---

[5] It is told of Costanzo Porta, the composer of Cremona, for example, that when in Padua he saw for the first time a copy of Zacconi's *Prattica di musica* which appeared in 1592, he cried out in amazement: "Not for a thousand ducats would I have disclosed the secrets which this monk has revealed here."

zealous musical amateur and had sent Palestrina some pieces of his own composition for criticism. Palestrina's comments on them are, however, of a somewhat general character and are obviously in agreement with Zarlino's doctrines. But this does not mean that Palestrina took them over from the works of that great theorist.[6]

But even this paucity of comment is not by any means remarkable, for history has demonstrated that great composers are often only mediocre theorists, that men who display in practice an astounding independence and boldness in their style are often remarkably naïve and helpless in theory, uncritically teaching rules that they have in their time found available in some book or other and for the most part restricting themselves merely to generalities.

Porta

Neither Palestrina nor the other great masters of that period wrote theoretical works. There are, however, in the Liceo Musicale of Bologna —which possesses one of the richest and choicest music libraries of the world—a few hitherto entirely unnoticed manuscripts of theoretical content, which come from important composers of the Palestrina style. One of these is a manuscript of the sixteenth century designated as instruction given by Costanzo Porta (1530 to 1601) to a certain Pater Tomasso Gratiano of Bagnacavallo. It begins with a discussion of the intervals and follows with a survey of consonances and dissonances. Then follows the usual section on the movement of perfect consonances into imperfect, of imperfect into perfect, of perfect into perfect, and so on, with some subsequent remarks on initial idioms and cadences and on the succession of note values. A whole note is best followed by a half, and this in turn by a quarter. A quarter can, however, also follow a whole, but in such a case it had best be dotted. For the rest, the material is put together somewhat helter-skelter and includes a colorful mixture of everything imaginable—circle-canons, ecclesiastical modes, interval progressions, rules of notation, mensural theory, and so on. The treatise contains practically nothing really new or remarkable; rules such as those given here can be found in other contemporary or earlier theorists more clearly and systematically presented.

---

[6] See my study: "Ueber einen Brief Palestrinas," *Festschrift zum 60. Geburtstag von Peter Wagner.* Leipzig, 1926. p. 100.

Giovanni Maria and Bernardino Nanini

The situation is somewhat similar in another manuscript also preserved in Bologna and attributed to the two brothers Giovanni Maria and Bernardino Nanini, famous composers who lived in Palestrina's time and are said to have been closely associated with him. Although this manuscript as a whole is not remarkable, it does contain some passages which are surprising in their independence. Here, perhaps for the first time, we come across the rule that two quarters may not occur alone in the place of the accented half notes in a measure. We find also several other important melodic-rhythmic rules which apparently are not stated elsewhere until later in the seventeenth century: for example, the rule that a stepwise progression in quarters should, so far as possible, be continued until it comes to an accented half note; on the other hand, it is not so good if such a movement in quarters ends on an unaccented half unless the latter is tied over and becomes a syncopation. The manuscript also states a rule that, so far as possible, one or two steps of a second downward should follow an ascending skip of a fourth, fifth, or octave. So far as I know, therefore, here is stated for the first time, though in a most primitive way, the important law concerning proper balance of the melody. Furthermore, it is taught that an ascending or descending stepwise movement in quarters should not begin on the first beat in the measure; it is best to let these movements in quarters begin in the place of the unaccented halves.

If this manuscript really dates from the time of Palestrina, it is remarkable in that it repeatedly anticipates subjects which otherwise were never formulated and discussed until the theorists of the seventeenth century. By and large, however, there is no essential difference between this source and the other more official, theoretical works of the sixteenth century. There is therefore hardly any reason for assuming that practical musicians surpassed the real theorists in knowledge to a degree worth mentioning—granted that, in accordance with a tacit agreement, they published only the rougher working rules.

Zarlino

Although the contrapuntal teaching of the sixteenth century by no means encompassed the positive side of the contrapuntal problem, several things lead us to conclude that the peculiarities of the polyphonic type of composition were by no means unknown to the theorists.   For example, Zarlino, the most important theorist of the sixteenth century, declared repeatedly that harmony arose out of melodies sounding simultaneously. Also with regard to the concept of melody, he took more pains than any theorist before him—just as in general he treated all aspects of technique in a more fundamental way than they were ever treated before.   In the Palestrina style itself, as is well known, the rule held that only perfect, major, and minor intervals could be used in melodies, and that all these intervals up to the fifth could be used without restriction in both directions.   Also the octave could be used, both ascending and descending, while all other skips, with the exception of the minor sixth ascending, were forbidden.   Of this rule, Zarlino writes as follows: [7]

The octave, fifth, fourth, and third can be used, as well as the tenth, which Josquin uses (as a matter of fact he uses the twelfth in "Inviolata").   One likewise uses dissonances such as the minor and major second.   It is true that occasionally, but very infrequently, ninth and sevenths are used, as one has observed in good masters and still can observe today.   One should, however, as is the practice with modern composers, avoid using the augmented fourth, the diminished fifth, and similar intervals.

One sees at once that Zarlino, whose work first appeared in 1558, deals principally with the practice of the Netherland composers as it developed during the first half of the sixteenth century in Italy, and that he does not present the actual set of rules of the Palestrina style.   That is something he could not do at that time for obvious reasons.   For example, with these earlier composers, such a freer treatment of the melody with larger skips was not unusual, while it is extremely rare in the compositions of Palestrina and his contemporaries.   It is worth noting that Zarlino says nothing concerning the possibility of using the minor sixth, but the rule for its use is already to be found in the famous work of the Swiss theorist Glarean, in the *Dodecachordon,* which otherwise is valuable more as a collection of examples.   What Zarlino and the later theorists of the century have to say about the finer melodic relations is in no wise striking. As a rule they restrict themselves to generalities, such as Zarlino's assertion that the voices should progress quietly and stepwise, because the beauty of the composition largely depends upon this method.   The requirement

---

[7] Zarlino, G., *L'Istitutioni harmoniche,* Tutte l'Opere. . . . Venice, 1589. Vol. I, pp. 251 ff.

that stepwise movement predominate is based chiefly upon the idea that such a treatment produces something which is easier to sing. Artusi says, for example, that melodies should move stepwise so far as possible because this method is in accord with nature and at the same time is convenient for the singer too; and in a contrapuntal work: *Dialogo del Don Pietro Pontio Parmigiano,* dating from 1595, which, according to a custom of the time, is arranged in the form of a dialogue, the pupil asks: "How should one proceed in order that singers may sing with ease and pleasure what one composes?"

To this question, the master replies: "By letting the parts proceed stepwise and in progressions from one harmony to another; by having proper, well-proportioned intervals." And Artusi follows a similar line of thought when he forbids the chromatic step because it confronts the singer with difficulties. In view of the decidedly vocal character of the art of this period, such a basis for the laws is quite comprehensible, but there is nevertheless a certain superficiality about it. The insistent demand for a voice leading that is stepwise and even, as far as possible, was doubtless based much more on a psychological than on any practical reason and may very well have been connected partly with the strong urge toward the simple and natural, which is characteristic of this century, and partly with an unconscious tendency to strengthen and fortify the polyphonic element as against the chordal, which is noticeably gaining in influence during the century.

If we turn now to the treatment of the dissonance, we will be surprised to observe that dissonances for the most part were still regarded chiefly as ornaments for consonances. What Zarlino thinks in this respect is characteristic: [8]

Although every composition, every counterpoint, indeed even every harmony is chiefly and preferably made up of consonances, one nevertheless uses dissonances too, although quite secondarily and incidentally (*per accidente*) in order to further the beauty and ornamentation—dissonances, which, although they sound somewhat unpleasant standing alone, are not only bearable but actually refresh and please the ear if they are introduced in a suitable and lawful manner. These dissonances afford the musician two (among other) advantageous possibilities of significant value: the first is that a dissonance may aid one to progress from one consonance to another; the second advantage is that dissonances heighten the pleasure of the consonances which follow immediately after them, just as light is much more pleasant and lovely to the

---

[8] Zarlino *op. cit.,* p. 212.

eye if it follows darkness, and just as something mild seems so much better and sweeter after something bitter.   Experience teaches us that the ear which is hurt by a dissonance finds the consonance which immediately follows so much the more charming and beautiful.   For this reason the musicians of old were of the opinion that not only perfect and imperfect consonances should be used in their compositions, but dissonances as well; they realized that the beauty of their compositions could be enhanced by the use of the latter.   Compositions which are made up solely of consonances may themselves sound good and have a beautiful effect; but there is something imperfect about them both melodically and harmonically in that the charm which may arise from the use of contrast is lacking.   And although I have said that one should for the most part use consonances in composition and that dissonances should be used only secondarily and more incidentally, one must not therefore assume that the latter can be used without any rule or order, for from this use only confusion would arise.

With respect to the treatment of dissonances, Zarlino's chief rule is that they may not occur in note-against-note writing or on the accented part of the measure, because they are too obtrusive there.   Ordinarily the half note is the longest value which may form a dissonance, and yet this is admissible only on the weak beat (hence on the second and fourth half notes in a measure), and there it is permissible only in conjunct motion. That is to say, if the dissonance is approached and quitted stepwise and in the same direction.   But half-note dissonances that move by skip are not allowed at all.   For quarter notes approximately the same rules apply as for half notes.   In a progression by skip only consonances may be used; on the other hand, if the movement progresses by step the unaccented quarters (that is, the second, fourth, sixth, and eighth quarters) may be dissonances.

Vicentino expresses this most briefly and clearly: [9]

In composition one ordinarily uses a consonance as the first quarter in a measure, a dissonance as the second, a consonance as the third, and a dissonance again as the fourth.   Where, however, only two quarters occur, and where these follow a syncopated whole note or a half note and the progression moves in a descending direction, the second and not the first of these two quarters must be a consonance; if, on the other hand, the movement is ascending, the first quarter must be consonant, the second dissonant.

Artusi, Tigrini, Ravn, and Sweelinck

What Zarlino and Vicentino teach with respect to the treatment of the dissonance is supplemented by Artusi as follows: [10] "In stepwise motion,

---

[9] *L'Antica musica ridotta alla moderna prattica* (1555), p. 32 v.
[10] *L'Arte del contraponto* (1598), p. 56.

composers commonly write two quarters as dissonances (in immediate succession) and thereby obtain an excellent effect." Oratio Tigrini, a canon of Arezzo who in 1588 published an excellent work, *Compendio della musica,* writes: [11] "Practical musicians, if they have to make any kind of a cadence with the use of four quarters, ordinarily arrange them in such a way that the third quarter forms a dissonance." Apart from some explanatory examples which follow, Tigrini gives us only the most meager information. He states merely that idioms of this sort are in general use and that Artusi regards the succession of two dissonances (second and third quarters) as the most remarkable feature of the combination. Tigrini does make the interesting observation, however, that we find this use of the accented quarter-note dissonance chiefly in cadences. The Danish music theorist Hans Mikkelsen Ravn (Corvinus), who in 1646 published a well-written but not especially original work on music theory, *Heptachordum danicum,* apparently bases his observations on Artusi. At any rate, he writes, "In stepwise motion the first and last quarters are consonant." He then introduces some explanatory examples which are quite in accord with Artusi, but which he apparently took directly from the *Compositionsregeln Herrn M. Johan Peterssen Sweeling,* the work of the famous Dutch organ composer Sweelinck, a pupil of Zarlino. Here the example which corresponds is given in connection with the statement: "Thus one may make both of the middle quarters bad, but the first and the last must be good." But this rule, which is based upon rather superficial considerations, is apparently much older; at any rate we find it already in Pietro Aron's *Toscanella in musica,* a work which appeared in 1523 in Venice. Here the relation between consonance and dissonance is stated in a most remarkable manner; the author requires that the first and last of the four notes which may follow either a breve or a whole note must be consonant, though the two middle notes may be dissonant.

The Seventeenth Century: Some Pedagogical Developments

Cerone

We obtain really satisfactory information on quarter-note dissonances only much later, through the Italian Pietro Cerone, who for a number of

---

[11] Page 33.

years was a singer at the court chapel at Madrid, and who in 1613 published in Spanish his epoch-making work, *El Melopeo,* a work that is imposing not merely because of its size. We find in it an almost overwhelming abundance of excellent observations as well as valuable information about the use of dissonances on the third of four quarters. Concerning this matter Cerone writes: [12]

> Only in cases where the part moves downward conjunctly in four quarters and where these quarters introduce a cadential device, is it permissible for the first and fourth quarters to be consonant while the second and third are dissonant. One should notice especially that under such circumstances all four quarters must move stepwise downward and also that the note which follows the fourth and last quarter is the upper second to this.

Cerone's rules are almost perfectly in accord with the laws which are observed in the Palestrina style: stepwise descending movement of four quarters and then a step of the second upwards, which gives the following melodic idiom: 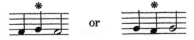 . Nevertheless, even Cerone's observation is not entirely exhaustive, for in actual practice the figure just cited almost always occurs in combination with a suspension dissonance in one of the other parts. Cerone mentions, just as Tigrini does, that the particular form of the quarter-note dissonance referred to occurs only in cadences; that he is not thinking here exclusively of cadential formulas with suspensions, however, is sufficiently evident from the musical examples given.

Otherwise with respect to the treatment of quarters as dissonances, it is remarkable that the so-called auxiliary notes,[13] which are unusually common in practice, receive only slight attention from the theorists. For the most part they are not mentioned at all; when any theorist does mention them, he usually merely forbids them. Of the following idioms, Artusi says it is best for the highest tone of the first, as well as the lowest

---

[12] *El Melopeo* (1613), p. 650.

[13] *Drehnoten*—I mean by this the device which consists of a "turning" with the upper or lower second and subsequent return to the principal tone, thus:

tone of the second, to be consonant, not dissonant as many seem to think.

It is further worth noting that the so-called anticipation dissonance (*Portamentodissonanz*)—which arises when an unaccented note approached from above is repeated (in which the dissonance normally can have only the duration of a quarter): —is not mentioned at all by the theorists, although it is everywhere in common use in the practical music of the sixteenth century. Still more remarkable, however, is the fact that one of the favorite devices of the fifteenth and sixteenth centuries, the so-called *cambiata,* is not discussed by any of the contemporary theorists and even in the seventeenth century does not seem to have been noticed. "*Cambiata*" is the name given to a figure which arises when an unaccented dissonant quarter, introduced by step from above, instead of continuing the conjunct motion downward, makes a skip of a third downward and is followed by a step of a second upward, thus reaching the tone of resolution, although late. As has been said, composers were very fond of using this device. Certain theorists, among whom was Angelo Berardi, who wrote in 1689, introduce various "*note cambiate,*" as Berardi calls them (literally, "changing notes"). He means by this term, however, chiefly figures like those previously mentioned in which the first of two descending quarters after an accented half forms a dissonance, or where the third of four quarters is a dissonance. So far as I know, the idiom with the skip of a third is especially designated as cambiata for the first time in 1725, the year in which the Austrian royal chapelmaster Johann Joseph Fux published his famous textbook on counterpoint, *Gradus ad Parnassum.* Concerning the treatment of eighth notes, the theory of the sixteenth century has nothing much to say, and concerning suspension-dissonances, the later theorists of this century say little more than Vicentino; about the forms of composition and the like, however, they do offer a great deal of information which is most significant in the study of the musical style of the Palestrina period but which does not directly affect the special problem of counterpoint.

In summary, the music theory of the sixteenth century by no means exhausts or covers contemporary practice. Indeed, one might say the same—perhaps with even more justification—about music theory of the twentieth century. One must marvel at the clarity and objectivity with which the time attempts to describe its music; in scarcely any other field was more straightforward, valuable scientific work accomplished. These dissertations are not, of course, textbooks in the modern sense, for special pedagogical concern is yet too much in the background—a situation unchanged till the development of the teaching of the "species" in the next century.

In the sixteenth century, as has been said, two movements made themselves felt. The first was a *musica comuna* based rather upon the past. Especially evident in the music of the church, it found its most distinguished representative in Palestrina. The second movement was the secular music and that church music which was more strongly influenced by the madrigal, with its clearly emphasized expressive tendencies. The latter movement prepared the way for the music of the seventeenth century with its new forms: the opera, the solo-cantata, the concerto, and others.

There has been a tendency to regard the events which took place about 1600 as a radical revolution in music. But they were revolutionary rather in their tendencies than in their initial manifestations. The musical situation at the end of the sixteenth century and the beginning of the seventeenth reveals, upon closer examination, a comparatively even transition from one musical style to another.

The decisive factor really appeared at the beginning of the sixteenth century, when the need for making music serve the ends of poetic expression was first clearly manifested. This urge had no very striking results to show at first. At the beginning of the seventeenth century, however, it received a renewed, decisive strengthening from without, from the realm of literature. The opera was created—a dramatic form which in the beginning used a kind of music as inadequate to express what was desired as the madrigal music of the sixteenth century. The will, however, was present and persisted until finally, after gaining sufficient mastery over the musical means of expression, it attained its goal: a subjective music able to give expression to the feelings and passions of the individual.

This development was made possible in many ways: first, through the removal of the strict treatment of dissonances according to law, further by replacing the artistic polyphonic weaving of the voices of the preceding time with a more chordal style. The old ecclesiastical modes were replaced by the major and minor scales. The feeling for tonal combinations became more refined, a sharper distinction was made between vocal and instrumental writing, and shorter note values, more energetic movements, and stronger rhythmic accents were introduced.

Berardi

Doubtless the reason the theorists clearly comprehend the trend of this whole development so quickly is that the time was ripe for it. Thus relatively early, in 1689, we find, for example, in a theoretical work, *Miscellanea musicale,* by the previously mentioned canon Angelo Berardi of Viterbo, a historical survey which in my opinion is better oriented concerning what was then essential in the situation than most modern discussions of it. Berardi writes:

Two styles of music are in use today: the first is based upon Plato's words: music is master of the text; the second style is that to which modern music belongs, but the situation is reversed, for here music is servant of the text. This music is called the second practice because consonances and dissonances had to be used other than those used in the practice of earlier composers. In their compositions, our predecessors have, for example, never used dissonant intervals such as diminished fifths, the tritone, and other dissonances. These, recently introduced in the second practice, make possible new effects which are necessary to express the words and which, if used in appropriate places, are free of all banalities, as works of various famous composers attest. Monteverdi in the "Lament of Arianna," for example, introduces with the opening words *"Lasciate mi morire"* ("Let me die"), the diminished fourth in a way effectively designed to arouse the sympathy of the listener. And Nenna (the madrigalist Pompeo Nenna) uses the same interval in the first of his four-part madrigals at the word *"umilita"* ("humility"). Cipriano de Rore uses the augmented fourth in his madrigal *"Poiche m'invitta amore"* at the words, *"Dolce mia vita"* ("My sweet life!"), and Giaches de Wert employs the same interval in the madrigal *"Misera non"* at the word *"essangue"* ("lifeless"); in addition Luca Marenzio and other excellent masters use them, as their works clearly indicate. And many examples can be found in which modern composers use the seventh, too, unprepared and accented. Modern musicians in general try to supplant the practice of former times, in that they seek to give impressive expression to the text in order better to arouse the feelings and passions of the listeners, as our predecessors were unable to do. Our predecessors employed only one and the same style and mode of treatment of consonances and dissonances, in all the works they published. If we turn, for example, to Palestrina, the prince and father of music, though by no means an especially old composer, we find only a slight difference between the style of his motets (sacred compositions) and that of his secular madrigals.

And if we examine these secular songs with French and Flemish texts, printed during 1545, 1546, 1549, 1550, and 1552 and composed by such masters as Crequillon, Janluys, Petit, Jean de Lattre, Baston, Clemens non Papa, Ricourt, Josquin, Adrian, Verdelot, and many other composers of various nations, we find here, too, very little difference between secular songs and sacred compositions. One difference is that the movements of the former are somewhat more lively where the words are gay and playful, as in the songs "La bella Margarita," "La Girometta," and "La Battaglia" of Jannequin and Verdelot. If, however, the content of the text is serious, then there is little or no difference with respect to style and the treatment of consonances and dissonances between the masses and motets of these masters and their madrigals. From this it is obvious that the earlier composers knew only one way of writing, one style, and that they used it for sacred as well as secular music. Modern composers have at their disposal, on the other hand, three style-species: a style for religious music, a style for domestic music, and a dramatic style for the theater. And yet there are, as has been said, two kinds of practice (two chief style-species): in the first music is the master of the text, but in the second the servant of the text.

Berardi goes as far as this. But it is somewhat surprising that, in spite of his clear conception of the difference between the music of his own time and that of the preceding century, the rules of counterpoint which he formulated should be almost identically the same as those of the theorists of the sixteenth century. Berardi's rules of counterpoint, therefore, have very little to do with the new practice, of which he seems otherwise such a zealous supporter. The same is true not only of Berardi, but also of all theorists of the seventeenth century: they preach the new but hold fast to the old. Only occasionally one or another of the musical idioms of their own time creeps into their musical examples—probably without intention. We face a *contrast between theory and practice* doubtless unparalleled in the earlier or later history of music. Yet we should probably be taking this relation too seriously, if we were to assume some conscious process of reasoning at the root of the matter. The explanation is conceivable, however, that the theorists of the seventeenth century believed the new style, in spite of its otherwise valuable characteristics, not well adapted to pedagogical uses. Or perhaps the explanation lies in the general human tendency to resist change, in inertia. In the course of the sixteenth century, contrapuntal theory had attained so solid an organization that it was not to be cast aside casually; if necessary it could continue to exist for a time independent of practice.

Although we find, in the seventeenth century, for the most part the same contrapuntal rules as in Zarlino, Vicentino, and Artusi, there is a new element in the way the teaching system itself was worked out. This new element brings the theorists of that time into a much more intimate relationship with what we now regard as counterpoint, from a pedagogical viewpoint.

The Cantus Firmus and the Species

For modern musicians *counterpoint* as a pedagogical term is closely associated with the idea of a cantus firmus and the "species." So far as the cantus firmus is concerned, we find this idea not only in the seventeenth century but also in the theorists of earlier times. Originally it was not motivated by pedagogical considerations, but was taken over into theory without further deliberation because it played a very important rôle in the earlier polyphony. Closely related to the innermost nature of music, it embodies one of the oldest and most profound musical ideas. The following rule may be set up as a primary law in the evolution of music: from a certain form A, one arrives at a new form B, by varying A gradually until finally it is so far varied that it becomes the new form B. From this viewpoint one may, with a certain justification, regard all music up to this time, after a thousand years of continuous modification, as a gigantic process of variation. It is an unending chain of variations, all naturally standing in more or less obvious relation to the theme, but all having one thing in common, namely, the visible or invisible, actual or ideal cantus firmus, to which they are linked and upon which they continue to build. Polyphony itself is based upon this principle of variation in one of its most primitive forms, the so-called heterophony (which in the evolution of our music lies before the time from which the examples of polyphony are transmitted to us). In heterophony there arises a certain rather accidental kind of polyphony when several voices sing the same melody simultaneously while each singer or instrumentalist varies the melody according to his inclination. And in the previously mentioned organum, which is the oldest western European form of polyphony preserved for us, the compositions are built up by adding one or more upper parts to a Gregorian melody. This principle of construction is retained in the motet writing of the twelfth and thirteenth centuries; indeed its influence is strongly felt until well into the fifteenth century. The cantus firmus—whether it is now an ecclesiastical melody or a folk song—occurs generally in the tenor but occasionally in one of the other voices. And for a long time, in fact until the *ordinarium* compositions of the sixteenth century, this principle was strongly felt, but here the cantus firmus technique is often of a more ideal character. For example, one no longer felt obliged to give to a single voice the sole right to the cantus firmus, but allowed all voices in succession to use certain motives taken from this basic melody. Hence it was not at all remarkable that the theorists of the Middle Ages should accept this technique (which thus has its deeper basis in the fact that music displays a certain gravitating tendency and inertia in its evolution and adheres to its first principles with remarkable tenacity). On the other hand, it is more remarkable that this technique can assert itself within contrapuntal theory and that it is retained when composers only rarely treat the cantus firmus in such an obvious manner. Meanwhile it is quite significant that *contrapuntal theory is in the process of changing from a discipline concerned with describing a style as best it can to one which emphasizes pedagogical ends.* Contrapuntal theory is not content merely to formulate the rules which it observes in practice or which it thinks it observes there; it begins to consider methods which will lead growing composers quickly and thoroughly to the mastery of the technique of music, methods particularly useful to them in practice. It is no longer sufficient to describe the technique of the great composers and then let the students imitate these models as best they can. Special exercises involving special difficulties are devised which are not taken from actual music, but which are designed to attain the goal more quickly. These attempts appear most clearly in the system of "species."

A common, popular conception of counterpoint is to think that it is identical with the "five species." Here the means is confused with the end; but it shows how closely the teaching of species has become entwined in the last centuries with the definition of counterpoint. At present nearly every textbook of counterpoint divides the material according to species. However much the views of the different authors may diverge, they do agree, with very few exceptions, in the teaching of the species.

The Eighteenth Century: The Style of Bach

Fux and the Species

This principle of division, with a motivation similar to that of more recent textbooks, we find first in the famous *Gradus ad Parnassum*. The author of this book, published in Vienna in 1725 by royal subsidy, was the highly respected composer, Johann Joseph Fux. This book is still used for instructional purposes in the editions of Bellerman, Haller, and others, where it has been changed in less essential points. Its practical significance, which no other work on contrapuntal theory has attained, is due not only to the pedagogically excellent arrangement of the material so that the difficulties increase gradually, but also partly to the fact that Fux was one of the first to take a more modern attitude toward counterpoint. The earlier theorists either concentrate on the practice of their own time or, perhaps in accordance with long-established custom, follow the theories of their predecessors without considering contemporary practice. Fux, however, was fully aware that one is confronted with a choice in the matter of music theory; one does not learn everything of significance from any one style-species. Every style has its particular technique and therefore one must know exactly why he chooses some particular style rather than another as the basis of instruction. Most of the theorists of the sixteenth and seventeenth centuries, without giving the matter further consideration, based their work on the music about them and only occasionally made some comment to the effect that this or that idiom is beautiful or modern or that another is old-fashioned or less usable. Fux, however, leaves the music of his own time, the Bach-Händel epoch, and chooses consciously and with clear foresight the music of Palestrina as the basis of his teaching. This is certainly not merely a matter of the conservatism of older people—Fux was sixty-five years old when he wrote the *Gradus ad Parnassum*—for Fux belongs by no means to the reactionaries who hold on with tooth and nail to what was the law in their youth, even though he speaks sharply about contemporary music, which, as he writes in the German edition of his book, "has almost become perverse." He is in fact a free spirit, a man who thinks practically and independently, who recognizes the weaknesses of his own time to the minutest detail and who seeks an effective remedy. But Fux's superiority has often been unrecognized. The German theorist of the Period of Enlightenment, Kirnberger, in 1782 wrote a study called *Gedanken über die verschiedenen Lehrarten in der Komposition* (*Thoughts on the Various Methods of Teaching Composition*) in which he criticizes Fux's procedure on the ground that it is too "strict" (*rein*). Kirnberger examines Fux's method in connection with the music of his own time and rejects it because it does not correspond. Later theorists even to our own time have repeated the same objections.

Fux therefore chooses the style of Palestrina as his basis, and in a very demonstrative manner indeed: in his preface he calls Palestrina "that splendid light in music to whom I owe everything I know of this science." Even if Fux's desire to learn and the will to master the teaching of Palestrina is stronger than his ability to do so, and although he intermixes elements of his own contemporary music in his discussions —quite possibly without realizing it—nevertheless his *Gradus* is on the whole still a valuable work, especially with respect to division and organization of the material.

Fux proceeds, as I have said, by steps from simple to complex, from easier to more difficult. He begins the practical part of his book with two-part counterpoint, and eventually goes on to three- and four-part counterpoint, and then to imitation, to the fugue, and to double counterpoint. For each particular kind of writing, two-, three-, and four-part, he sets up the same five exercises or species. In the first species he adds an upper part, then a lower part in whole notes to the cantus firmus, so that the counterpoint moves "note against note" in the form called in the preceding centuries *contrapunto semplice*. Fux here teaches the same principle taught in earlier times, that dissonances may not be used in this species at all. But he does not proceed, as was the custom of the theorists of the fifteenth and sixteenth centuries, directly from simple counterpoint, note against note, to that with motion, the so-called counterpoint by diminution in which different note values and rhythms are used in an entirely free manner. Instead Fux continues quite systematically and in the second species sets two half notes to each whole note in the cantus firmus. Dissonances are admitted in this species only on the unaccented portion of the measure, and then only if they are treated as passing notes. In the third species, consequently, four quarters are written against each whole note in the cantus firmus. Here the weak quarters, the second and fourth notes of each measure, may dissonate just as in the second species—as passing notes. In Fux's opinion the third quarter may be dissonant provided both of the quarters which adjoin it on either side are consonant. Where Fux found this rule I do not know; possibly he formulated it himself. At any rate it is not based upon the practice of the Palestrina style. In this species, furthermore, Fux mentions, apparently for the first time in music theory, the *cambiata*. In the fourth species again only half notes are used, but this time as suspensions. Every unaccented half is tied over to the succeeding accented note. These accented half notes introduced by ties may dissonate, but then they must descend stepwise to the following unaccented portion of the measure. Finally the fifth species is the so-called *contrapunctus floridus* ("flowering" counterpoint) and corresponds to the *contrapunto diminuto* of the earlier theorists. Fux introduces here no particularly detailed rules but he does observe that two isolated quarters may occur in the place of an accented half note only under certain restrictions.

This rhythmical arrangement of the species is, however, not Fux's invention. The beginnings of this procedure are found toward the end of the sixteenth century. *Il Transilvano* (1597), a well-known theoretical work by Girolamo Diruta, for the first time treats counterpoint in half notes (that is, the second species of Fux). After that comes counterpoint in syncopated halves and then in quarters, and finally exercises with mixed note values.

In Adriano Banchieri's *Cartella musicale,* a work which appeared in 1614 in Venice, we find almost exactly the same arrangement of the species as in Fux: first, counterpoint in note against note, then two halves against each whole note of the cantus firmus; after that, four quarters, then syncopated half notes. However, in place of the "fifth species," Banchieri mentions the so-called *contrapunto fugato*. This name implies that the contrapuntal part imitates and obviously attempts to produce the illusion of a fugue in that it introduces a theme which is answered in the fifth later in the same part. Then follows the *contrapunto ostinato,* in which the contrapuntal part has complete rhythmic freedom within the limits of a melodic motive, an ascending scale of six tones, which therefore must be rhythmically varied so that it conforms at all times to the cantus firmus.

Finally, Zacconi's *Prattica di musica* (1622), an excellent and more comprehensive work, introduces in the second part all the Fux species in exact order: whole notes, halves, quarters, syncopations, and mixed values.   In addition to these five species, Zacconi has a large number of other exercises: examples for counterpoint in which only stepwise movement may occur and for counterpoint in just the opposite manner, in which only skips are allowed; examples for *imitatione per diretto,* where a scalewise descending motion is answered after the manner of the fugue in one and the same voice, and for *imitatione per contrario,* in which a descending scalewise progression is imitated in the inversion (likewise in the same part); and a number of other similar species.   This tendency to think up artificial, difficult exercises seems to grow in the course of the seventeenth century.

In one of the most representative works of this century on the theory of music, the *Documenti armonici* of Angelo Berardi, who has been mentioned before, we find, for example, a countless number of such tricks, which may possibly have stimulated the imagination of the pupil but which were otherwise hardly of great value.   Berardi begins with the *contrapunto alla zoppa* ("limping" counterpoint) in which the rhythm ♩ ♩ ♩ is maintained strictly.   Then Berardi presents counterpoint in

stepwise, progression, in which skips may not occur at all, and finally a "skipping" counterpoint in which stepwise movement is forbidden.   In the next chapter he introduces counterpoint in which a single note value, the dotted half note, is used and follows this with counterpoint which

maintains the following rhythm throughout: ♩. ♪♩. ♪.   He next

treats counterpoint which moves exclusively in the rhythm: ♩ ♩. ♪♪♪ and many other kinds of invariable rhythms.   Berardi tells further, as does Banchieri, of *contrapunto fugato* and *ostinato* and in addition of counterpoint in which certain intervals such as fifths, octaves or tenths are forbidden; of counterpoint in free note values in which dissonances may not occur at all; of counterpoint in ternary measure; and of counter-

point *in saltarello,* which moves in a certain dance rhythm: ♩. ♩ ♩

In short, his power of invention is almost inexhaustible.   However colorful and confused all this may seem and however little significance in contrapuntal instruction one may be inclined to attribute to it, the tendency here manifested deserves attention; it gives evidence of a certain urge toward pedagogical arrangement of the material on the part of the theorist. The examples which they introduce in their books are no longer taken directly from actual compositions but constructed by the respective authors themselves. Obviously no composer writes a composition of any length which progresses, for example, exclusively in halves or quarters. And yet it may be quite appropriate that the pupil should at first disregard rhythmical problems and concentrate completely upon the treatment of the melodic line and the dissonance so that the further difficulties, which arise out of the combination of rhythms, are allowed to come up only after he has fully mastered these. It would likewise be difficult to find compositions in which the voices move stepwise exclusively; and yet one may conclude with some justification that the practice of counterpoint which employs only conjunct motion and mastery of this way of writing builds a reserve which will help a composer to write a very free, flowing, even melody to a cantus firmus.

It cannot be denied, however, that many entirely superfluous exercises and theoretical trifles were introduced in textbooks of the seventeenth century; not until Fux takes the matter in hand, reducing the species to five and increasing the difficulties successively, is a form evolved which is really practical for pedagogical purposes.

With the first half of the eighteenth century, therefore, the primitive stage of contrapuntal theory is left behind. One no longer writes down without reservation or critique the rules which he observes or believes he observes in practice, but he begins to reason about them and to stylize them if he considers this desirable; he selects and rejects. The situation is, to be sure, a much more complicated one than that in the sixteenth century. In the interim an art has developed which has definitely, almost exclusively, a harmonic basis. As a result, in musical theory there has arisen an entirely new discipline: the *thoroughbass system* of instruction, which develops within a short time into the *theory of harmony,* with its complementary concept, *counterpoint.* Therefore, in describing music, one must choose between the two methods where formerly there was no choice.

Along with this development, polyphonic music attained its second climax in the first half of the eighteenth century with Johann Sebastian Bach. We are faced with a further choice in contrapuntal theory: Bach or Palestrina? From now on contrapuntal theory divides in two directions; and although most theorists have decided in favor of Palestrina, Bach is not wanting in followers, among whom are many important personalities. One of the first theorists, possibly the first, to follow Bach was Kirnberger.

Kirnberger

Johann Philipp Kirnberger, who studied with Bach in Leipzig, retained throughout his life the deep impression which he received from the personality of the great master; in fact he even seemed somewhat ridiculous to his contemporaries because of the obvious fanaticism with which he defended everything pertaining to Bach's honor and greatness. His critique of every art other than Bach's was harshly derogatory, yet he did not seem to have a truly critical judgment himself. Only the positive aspects of his theories are of real value. The attacks in his *Grundgedanken über die verschiedenen Lehrarten in der Komposition* directed against Berardi, Bononcini, and Fux, who in his opinion are responsible for the best and purest works on the theory of music, consist of a series of objections that have little point. Berardi's style displays unity and character, but it is not to be recommended because of its very strict viewpoint. Besides, he does not discuss various more modern advances in music. Bononcini, to be sure, may be less limited in his style, but he does not take care that the character of the initial theme dominates the whole composition. Finally, so far as Fux is concerned, Kirnberger finds that his rules are too strict and that his textbook too quickly takes up the fugue, which Kirnberger also regarded as by far the most difficult form of composition. Kirnberger's critique is obviously lacking in mature reflection. He assumes quite as a matter of course that the Bach style is the only right one; if the earlier theorists do not agree with this style then their teaching has thereby condemned itself. On the other hand, Kirnberger writes concerning his great teacher:

Johann Sebastian Bach uses a thoroughly pure style in all his compositions; every work of his has a definite unified character. Rhythm, melody, harmony, in short, all that makes a composition really beautiful, he has completely at his command as is attested by his works. His method is the best, for he makes the transition from the easiest to the most difficult step by step in a thorough manner, and for this very reason the step to the fugue itself is no more difficult than any of the other steps on the way. For this reason I consider *the method of Johann Sebastian Bach the one and only method*. It is to be regretted that this great man never wrote anything theoretical about music and that his teachings have come down to posterity only through his pupils. I have attempted to reduce the method of the late Johann Sebastian Bach to its basic principles and, in my *Kunst des reinen Satzes,* to reveal his teachings to the world to the best of my ability.

The work which Kirnberger mentions here really contains such an attempt, and comparison between the result here and the earlier contrapuntal theory may therefore be of interest.

As usual, Kirnberger begins with an acoustical exposition of the tonal material and of intervals. Then he brings in some sections on chords in which he discusses the different forms and inversions of the triads and chords of the seventh and gives rules for their treatment. He also mentions the dissonant suspension. Because the dissonances brought about in this manner can be omitted without causing a mistake or a lack of clearness, Kirnberger calls them "unessential" dissonances. On the other hand he characterizes as "essential" those dissonances which occur in a chord, as for example the seventh of the chord of the seventh. Kirnberger writes in great detail about the treatment of both essential and unessential dissonances, about harmonic periods and cadences, about modulation into nearly related and more distant keys, about harmonic and inharmonic (consonant and dissonant) skips in melodies. Moreover, he discusses in general the whole material ordinarily included in a system of harmony, before passing on in the tenth chapter to the discussion of the problem which he calls simple counterpoint in two or more parts. And we find rather early in this section a remark characteristic of Kirnberger:

Simple strict counterpoint can be in two, three, four, or more parts. It is best to begin with four-part counterpoint because it is hardly possible to write in two or three parts perfectly until four-part writing has been mastered. For since the complete harmony is in four parts, something must always be missing in two- and three-part works, so that one cannot judge safely as to what is to be omitted from the harmony in the different cases which arise unless he has a thorough knowledge of four-part writing.

With one stroke this remark actually discloses the whole transformation which took place in the polyphonic art during the seventeenth and eighteenth centuries. Kirnberger no longer begins with the line, as did his predecessors, but with the chord; and yet he wants polyphony. But here he is entirely in the right because the polyphony he is striving for is the harmonically conceived linear music of the late baroque, of the Bach style. His complete break with the practice up to that time, which began with two-part counterpoint and gradually increased the number of voices, and his departure in an almost diametically opposed direction give evidence throughout of logicality and of a vigorous power of observation. The reasons he gives for this break are most significant: for him the chord is primary; the interval is comprehensible only as a constituent of a chord. A third, for example, is an incomplete triad of which either the root or the fifth is missing; the "empty" fifth is "empty" because the intermediate third is lacking, which would make it a complete triad. From here it is actually only a step to the Riemann definition of the dissonance as simply a nonharmonic element.

Kirnberger now proceeds to describe first the four-part counterpoint in "note against note," then the three-part, and finally the two-part technique. The last-mentioned he designates, in connection with his earlier discussions, the most difficult of all the ways of writing, involving a technique impossible to master without an accurate knowledge of the four-part style. After this he discusses five- and six-part writing, and then proceeds to the so-called "ornamental" or "florid" counterpoint. By this he means the same form as that which the early contrapuntal theorists called *contrapunto diminuto* (hence, for example, the fifth species of Fux), and he divides this species into three groups, the first of which comprises the so-called chordal figuration, a technique completely foreign to the theory of the sixteenth century. The second group includes the so-called passing notes, which can be either regular or irregular; the former occur on weak accents, like the passing notes which we know from Fux and the Italian theorists, and generally fill out the intervals of a third which adjoin them on either side. But these can, in contrast to the practice of Palestrina's time, be approached and quitted by skips. By "irregular" passing notes Kirnberger means the accented passing dissonance, which is now called the appoggiatura dissonance. He is concerned here with an idiom which significantly differentiates the Bach polyphony from the Palestrina style (where such dissonances do not occur, at least not on the unequivocally accented portions of the measure). Where two or more voices progress simultaneously with passing notes, up to four dissonances may occur directly in succession provided the movement is lively and the melody easily understood. Yet here one will be wise to set to work somewhat cautiously. It is better, says Kirnberger, to follow Chapelmaster Graun in this matter than Händel or Johann Sebastian Bach, because Graun writes with the greatest of prudence and in vocal writing aims for the most harmonious combinations. Bach is more venturesome in this respect than anyone else; consequently his compositions require a very particular performance, one well suited to his way of writing, for otherwise listening to his works would often be unbearable on account of their harsh effects. One who does not understand harmony thoroughly should never play his more difficult works; on the other hand, if one is able to achieve the right sort of performance, even the most learned of his fugues sound excellent. Kirnberger here takes cognizance of a peculiar, essential side of the Bach technique, where, in spite of the decidedly chordal basic viewpoint, the linear elements come to the fore so strongly, so independently at certain times, that the harshness of the tonal combinations is understandable only through the logic of the voice leading. The third group which Kirnberger discusses is the so-called "uneven progression" (*"ungleiche Gang"*). By this term he means the relation in which two voices, originally intended to move simultaneously note against note, are separated by a reciprocal displacement, giving rise to a species of syncope, mostly in very small note values. With these discussions Kirnberger closes the first part of his book.

The second part begins with instruction concerning the four-part harmonization of a given soprano. Kirnberger then introduces a section on the various older and more modern modes and scales. The third chapter is especially interesting because it treats of melodic progression and of "flowing" melody. Kirnberger investigates first of all the tone with which a melody should begin in order that the mode may be recognized as quickly as possible. With regard to the further development of the melody he remarks that every good melody must have certain correct harmonies as a basis; melodies in which the harmonic foundation is not palpable and easily grasped cannot be flowing. Kirnberger's theory is here certainly most limited because of the time in which he lived, but it corresponds excellently with his whole basic conception. Very wisely he adds that one must not jump to the apparent corollary because not every melody which rests upon a clear and correct harmonic basis is necessarily successful. He further observes that smaller intervals, such as seconds and thirds, are better for the flowing progression of the melody than sixths, sevenths, octaves, and so on. The latter intervals, therefore, should be used only where a stronger accent is desired or where the smooth movement is abandoned in consideration of the expression. To express anger or joy, skips are most effective, but to express a more quiet mood, stepwise movement is best suited; but this kind of movement must not be carried to excess, because continued scalewise gliding up and down is monotonous and irksome. Melodies that continue for long periods with tones lying exclusively within one scale very easily become insipid; there is indeed only a hand's breadth between the flowing and the trivial. In order to obviate this sort of monotony, a tone foreign to the key should be woven in occasionally, especially if the chief accent of the passage is transferred to this particular tone.

Kirnberger then discusses in succession the melodic use of the different intervals without bringing in anything especially worth noting. He ends finally with a survey of the emotional effects of the intervals. This conclusion is in accord with the so-called theory of the emotions of the Period of Enlightenment. The augmented prime ascending, for example, tends to produce an effect of "anxiety"; descending, it is "most melancholy." The diminished seventh sounds "painful," the minor seventh "tender and melancholy, timid," the major seventh "violent, raving, full of despair"—all in ascending movement. Descending, the diminished seventh sounds "lamenting," the minor seventh "somewhat fearful," the major seventh "terribly fearful," and so on.

The fourth section of the second book deals with meter and rhythm and now and then introduces something really valuable and new. The two last and most extensive divisions finally discuss the subject of double counterpoint.

By way of summing up Kirnberger's work, one must say that in spite of all his thoroughness and ability he is able to draw out very little of the polyphonic values which lie hidden in Bach's incomparable art. The viewpoints upon which Kirnberger's work rests are often very nearly right. Bach, who in other respects seems to have recognized the Fux method,[14] apparently followed in the instruction of his personal pupils a method very similar to that described by Kirnberger. Both Kirnberger's statements and those of Philipp Emanuel Bach confirm the assumption that the great Johann Sebastian let his pupils begin contrapuntal instruction with the four-part harmonization of chorales only after they had worked through the whole of harmony. Bach, for example, let Heinrich Nikolaus Gerber, his pupil, first go through the inventions and then some suites and the "Well-Tempered Clavichord." Later he proceeded to the thoroughbass and gave Gerber the task of working out in four parts different basses from Albinoni's violin compositions. He used a similar procedure in the instruction of another pupil, Johann Friedrich Agricola, to whom he first gave practical instruction in organ and clavier playing, introducing him later to the study of harmony.

THE NINETEENTH CENTURY: PALESTRINA OR BACH?

The description of Bach's style was meanwhile not directly continued after Kirnberger. At the end of the eighteenth and the beginning of the nineteenth centuries, contrapuntalists depended chiefly on Fux. Haydn instructed the young Beethoven according to the *Gradus ad Parnassum*. The real progress in music theory consists of a more fundamental and more refined working out of the theory of harmony, which had already received decisive attention in Rameau's *Traité de l'harmonie* (1722).

Richter

A continuation of the work begun by Kirnberger appeared only with Ernst Friedrich Richter's *Lehrbuch des einfachen und doppelten Kontrapunkts*, which was published in 1872. Much earlier, in 1838, the Berlin Professor A. B. Marx had, in the second volume of his *Kompositionslehre*, treated the contrapuntal forms from the viewpoint of the Bach polyphony, although on a broader, more formal basis. Strangely enough, however, the newly awakened interest in Bach, which is one of the most significant features of the Mendelssohn generation, produced

---

[14] Ph. Spitta: *Johann Sebastian Bach.* Leipzig, Breitkopf und Härtel, 1873–1880. Vol. II, pp. 604–605.

no comprehensive works on Bach's style, possibly because of the slight rôle which strict polyphony generally played in the compositions of the romantic composers.

Richter uses to a certain extent the same method as Kirnberger. He assumes that the pupil has a complete mastery of harmony and begins with four-part writing, note against note. The chief rule here is that all chords, including the chords of the seventh and their inversions, may be used. Richter makes use of three species, coming closer in this respect to Fux than Kirnberger comes. The first of these species is "note against note"; in the second, two half notes are written against every whole note in the cantus firmus. On the accented portion of the measure, only consonant chords or suspension dissonances are permitted. On the unaccented beat passing dissonances may occur, but only so far as they are constituents of some seventh chord or other chord that is correctly treated. In such cases they may even be approached and quitted by skips, especially where the harmonic progression is relatively smooth. In third species Richter, like Fux, sets four quarters to each whole note in the cantus firmus. Here the first note in each measure must be a harmony note, yet in exceptional cases a suspension that is well treated or a changing note may occur instead of the chord tone. Otherwise passing or changing notes may be used anywhere, but always only with stepwise treatment. Richter's further species include counterpoint with three or six notes to each note in the cantus firmus. These additions are justified, since the objection can be raised against Fux that he neglects the ternary measure in accordance with the practice of the sixteenth century, a deficiency which the later revisions of the *Gradus* seek to remedy. In a similar manner Richter now treats the three-part and then the two-part counterpoint. Later on, the larger contrapuntal forms and double counterpoint follow.

Jadassohn, Riemann, Krehl

S. Jadassohn's *Lehrbuch des Kontrapunkts,* published in 1883, is drawn up in accordance with approximately the same principles. In comparison with Kirnberger, both Richter's and Jadassohn's works really represent a retrograde step, for through them one attains even less of the greatness of the Bach style than through Kirnberger's works. Moreover, they are vacillating in their method, intermixing the principles of the harmonically oriented counterpoint with those of the Palestrina style. The result is actually neither harmony nor counterpoint, but a vague, characterless, mongrel product.

Hugo Riemann, in his *Lehrbuch des Kontrapunkts,* which appeared in 1888, begins in the same way as Richter and Jadassohn, but he has a much better concept of the essence of the Bach style. For him, too, harmony is the hypothesis through which all the rules of voice leading of the earlier counterpoint textbooks are made superfluous; for he says:

> Two-part counterpoint knows only the laws which likewise govern four-part harmonic writing. But these laws must unconsciously guide the gift for melodic invention; the imagination must be able to move freely without reflection within the realm of the available possibilities.

Later Riemann remarks, however, that the possibility of a harmonic interpretation of a cantus firmus is for the most part very limited; indeed there is often the problem of finding the one and only possible solution. Here Riemann obviously has some apprehension lest the counterpoint should be too closely linked with harmonic considerations; therefore he would like to repress chordal feelings into the realm of the subconscious. Stefan Krehl, however, in his little handbook *Kontrapunkt* (1908), boldly ventures to draw the conclusion which Riemann here avoids. Krehl remarks that the pupil who proceeds from the thorough study of harmony to counterpoint becomes so accustomed to combining melody and harmony that he is really compelled to conceive the tones as representatives of certain chords. Therefore it is not particularly difficult for him to imagine the missing tones when he constructs a chord out of only two tones. Now, in order to produce the most favorable presentation or representation of the particular chord, every melody or cantus firmus to be treated must first be harmonized in four parts. In two-part writing, then, the problem is to select the tones which best and most clearly represent the harmony. But at the same time, proper attention must be paid to the voice leading. The placing of counterpoint on a harmonic basis could scarcely be formulated more clearly.

Yet it is remarkable that both Riemann and Krehl, in spite of such an attitude toward chords, follow exactly the same procedure as Fux;

that is, they begin with two-part counterpoint and gradually increase the number of voices. They also use the species with one, two, three, four, or six notes in the added part to each note of the cantus firmus. In both we see, moreover, a kind of atavism: both use the "rhythmized" counterpoint, in that every separate voice maintains its own particular, more complex kind of movement, just as in contrapuntal practice before Fux. After reading the works of Riemann and Krehl, we must admit that the former is right when, in an entirely different connection, he maintains that the more modern theory of music, in spite of all attempts, has not had the slightest success in making the laws of the Bach polyphony clear.

Kurth, Krohn, Grabner

One work, however, deserves to be mentioned in this respect, the previously mentioned book of Ernst Kurth: *Grundlagen des linearen Kontrapunkts*. This work is no textbook of music theory in the real sense, but rather a book dealing with style from a psychological and biological viewpoint. In his exposition, Kurth succeeds in presenting much of his unusual understanding of Bach's great boldness and power. He calmly creates an entirely new symbolism for the description of music and carries on more intensive work with melodic problems. His basic historical viewpoint is, however, essentially imperfect in that he has only one side of the Bach style in view, the linear, and he disregards or attempts to deny the unquestionable fact of its resting on a harmonic basis. With him we are for the time being at the end of the movement in contrapuntal theory which proceeds from Bach. And yet I should not like to omit mention of Ilmari Krohn's textbook on counterpoint (1927), which at present is unfortunately available only in Finnish. Krohn's work, based on Bach, reveals an alert understanding of the rhythmical problem and makes a noteworthy attempt to provide musical motivation of the exercises. H. Grabner's *Der lineare Satz* also adopts an interesting viewpoint. This book, which appeared at the same time as the original Danish edition of the present work (1930), is likewise characterized by an energetic emphasis on linear aims. In my opinion, however, the too indefinite stylistic background of the exposition does not permit the plasticity and penetration necessary in a textbook.

THE "PALESTRINA MOVEMENT" AFTER FUX

Martini, Cherubini, Bellermann

The "Palestrina movement" and its development record no important progress since Fux. Padre Martini, the great counterpoint teacher of the eighteenth century, has left no really didactic work. His *Saggio fondamentale pratico di contrappunto* (1774–76), although intelligently and interestingly annotated, is rather a collection of examples of vocal polyphony than an actual textbook of counterpoint. But the majority of the theorists of the eighteenth and nineteenth centuries follow Fux without important alterations in his teaching. A special place is occupied here by Cherubini's well-known *Cours de contrepoint,* which systematically adheres entirely to Fux with an occasional license in accordance with a more modern taste taking the form of some dissonances on the accented part of the measure. The *Gradus* experienced a revival in 1862 through Heinrich Bellermann's significant revision. The author enriched the work with varied material, chiefly of a historical nature, concerning notation, scales, and so on. Bellermann, however, does not come much closer to the real Palestrina style than Fux. He follows the Fux rules and, like his successors Haller, Hohn, and the rest, neglects to determine by investigation whether the rules in Fux are really those of Palestrina. This task is now before us; we cannot progress further in this field of contrapuntal theory until we know something about this question.[15]

If a brief review of the trend of contrapuntal development is made, we must conclude that everything that composers and theorists have created and imagined through diverse times may be traced to two basic ideas. One has been expressed most clearly by Zarlino: *"L'harmonia nasce dal cantare, che fanno insieme le parti delle cantilene"* (harmony arises from the simultaneous singing of melodies). The other was apparently first formulated by Rameau: *"La mélodie provient de l'harmonie"* (melody comes from harmony). This is the source of the two forms of polyphony and the theoretical disciplines associated with them. Both are justified, for both had temporary validity in the history of music.

---

[15] I should like to mention R. O. Morris's *Contrapuntal Technique in the Sixteenth Century* (Oxford, 1922) as a worthy work, although not really adapted for teaching purposes.

But from the historical-biological standpoint, doubtless only the first basic idea is sound: melody came first and only later was the way to harmony found.   And surely this is also the view which everyone must take who analyzes the nature of counterpoint.

Chapter II

TECHNICAL FEATURES

Notation

IN ADDITION TO the G clef on the second line (the "discant clef") and the F clef on the fourth line (the "bass clef"), which are in general use today, classical vocal polyphony makes considerable use of the C clef, which indicates the position of middle C on the staff. This clef could theoretically be used on any one of the five lines, but it is used most

frequently on the first line: 𝄡 ("soprano clef"), on the third line:

𝄡 ("alto clef") and on the fourth line: 𝄡 ("tenor clef"). The

C clef on the second line ("mezzo-soprano clef") 𝄡 was used less

frequently and is found only very rarely on the fifth line ("baritone clef"), since the F clef on the third line, which means the same thing, was generally preferred:

𝄡 ♩ = 𝄢 ♩ = 𝄢 ♩

This comparatively large selection of clefs, characteristic of the earlier music, was for the purpose of avoiding as much as possible the use of leger lines, which could easily make the note-picture vague and indistinct. It was preferable to change clefs and thus avoid having the notes too often exceed the limits of the five lines. It is to be regretted that these clefs have gradually gone out of use. The tenor clef especially is sorely missed, since neither the treble nor the bass clef is suited to the range of the tenor.   To note the tenor in the G clef an octave higher than it sounds always will be a miserable makeshift.   It is valuable in general for the musician to be accustomed to the C clefs, since they open to him the very great and sublimely beautiful *a cappella* literature.   They can also be of use to him in the matter of transposition.

In the vocal polyphony of the sixteenth century the following note values were used: maxima (large = eight whole notes): ; longa (long = four whole notes): ; brevis (breve = two whole notes): ; semibrevis (semibreve = one whole note): ◇ ; minima (minim = one half note): ; semiminima (semiminim = one crotchet or quarter note): ; and fusa (one quaver or eighth note): . The following rests correspond to these note values:

| Maxima | Longa | Brevis | Semibrevis | Minima | Semiminima |

In addition to these symbols of notation, certain so-called *ligatures* were used to indicate that the notes concerned were to be slurred and executed in one breath.   Although such ligatures are not used in the exercises in this book, the most important rules regarding their treatment are very briefly given here, since one must know them to become acquainted at first hand with the contrapuntal music of the fifteenth and sixteenth centuries.[2]

The ligatures are divided into two groups: *ligaturae rectae,* in which the quadrate notes are written close together, for example:

[1] Eighth rests are not used in the vocal polyphony of the sixteenth century.

[2] More detailed information on these questions will be found in Jacobsthal, *Die Mensural-notenschrift des 12. und 13. Jahrhunderts.* Berlin, Springer, 1871; H. Bellermann, *Die Mensural-noten und Taktzeichen des 15. und 16. Jahrhunderts.* Berlin, Reimer, 1906; and Johannes Wolf, *Handbuch der Notationskunde,* Vol. 1. Leipzig, Breitkopf und Härtel, 1913.

and *ligaturae obliquae,* where they are written with an oblique figure and in such a way that the beginning and end of this figure indicates the

two notes united in the ligature, for example:  .

The first note of every ligature is called *nota initialis,* the last, *nota finalis;* and the notes which may happen to lie in between are called *notae mediae.*

If the *nota initialis* has no descending *cauda* (tail) and if it is higher than the following note, then it has the value of a longa, regardless of

whether the ligature is *recta* or *obliqua:* 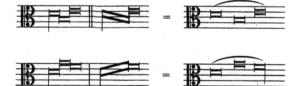 .

These two ligatures, therefore, mean the same: 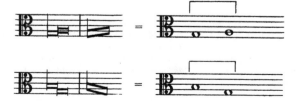 . If

the *nota initialis* has no *cauda* yet is lower than the following note, it counts as a breve whether *recta* or *obliqua:*

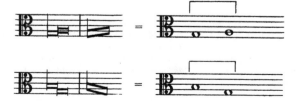

If, on the other hand, the initial tone has a line downward on the left side, then it counts as a breve whether the ligature is *recta* or *obliqua* or whether the following tone is higher or lower:

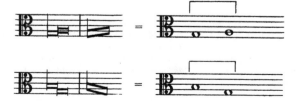

With a line upwards on the left side (*ligatura cum opposita proprietate*), the initial tone and the following tone each counts as a semibreve, whether the ligature is *recta* or *obliqua* or whether the motion is ascending or descending:

Here, however, another rule also comes into play, in accordance with which every note belonging to a ligature which has a tail extending upward on the right side counts as a breve, while a descending tail on the same side of the note gives it the value of a long, for example:

All *notae mediae,* that is all notes lying between the initial and final tones of a ligature, are breves, unless they are changed into semibreves as members of a *ligatura cum opposita proprietate* or given the value of a long by the descending stem on the right side.

The final tone of every *obliqua* counts as a breve:

In *ligaturae rectae,* too, the closing tone is a breve if it is higher than the preceding note; if it is lower, it is a long:

The use of *caudae* in ligatures may be briefly summarized:

1. A descending stem on the left side of the note gives it the value of a breve.

2. The ascending stem on the left side of the note makes this note and the following note semibreves.

3. If the note has a line downward on the right side it counts as a long, but if it has an ascending stem on the same side, it has the value of a breve.

The following examples show typical ligatures and their solutions:

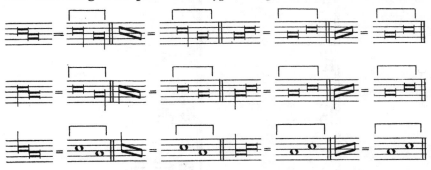

In the sixteenth century as in modern music, the dot meant the lengthening of the note by one-half its value; the double dot, however, was not used. But dotted rhythms could be indicated by filling in the normal white or open notes.

In such cases the following form of notation was most frequently used:

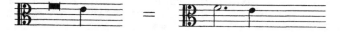

Besides the arrangement of the clefs which was most common in the sixteenth century: the following
may also
be found:

The latter arrangement was called *chiavette* or *chiavi trasportate* (transposition clef), and it was used to indicate that the particular composition could be performed a minor or a major third lower than actually noted. Thus if the first set of clefs in the following example is mentally replaced by the second and the proper key signature kept in mind, a transposition is easily effected.

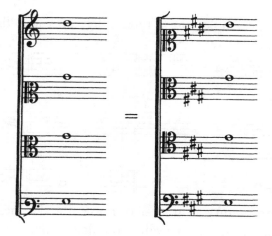

The Ecclesiastical Modes

The music of the sixteenth century is based upon the so-called ecclesiastical modes, a system of modes that existed in the music of western Europe from the origin of the Latin Church and dominated music until the seventeenth century, when the transition to our major-minor system, long under way, finally began to prevail.

The oldest practical evidence of the existence of the church modes we find in the Gregorian chants, in those time-honored melodies of the Catholic Church which apparently constitute the earliest art music produced by our Western culture.

The evolution of these modes was not brought about by solemn agreement upon certain forms to which composers of Gregorian melodies then had to adapt themselves, any more than spoken languages owe their origin to the establishment of an alphabet. In music as in all other fields, practice has preceded theory. The music of the church in the oldest form in which it has come down to us (and, at least so far as notation is concerned, this can scarcely go back further than the ninth or tenth century), affords clear evidence that the ecclesiastical modes were not, so to speak, *a priori* to it, and that we must rather regard them as certain principles of organization coming from without, with whose aid the attempt was made to bring, in the best way possible, some semblance of order to a material originally somewhat disorganized and intractable.

The fundamental principle of organization, which was called *oktoechos,* was founded upon a system of eight modes.

Originally only four modes were actually used. These were designated with the Greek numbers *protus* (the first), *deuterus* (the second), *tritus* (the third), and *tetrardus* (the fourth). Each of these four modes was later divided into two forms, a lower called *plagal* (derived) and a higher called the *authentic* form. In spite of having different ranges (the beginning tone of the plagal scale was always a fourth below that of the corresponding authentic), both modes had the same final.

The system of the eight modes seems to have appeared as early as the time of Pope Gregory the Great, who ruled from 590 to 604. The Gregorian chant was apparently named after him. Already at that time it had the form shown on the next page, which it has since retained:

First Mode
(authentic *protus*, later Dorian)

Second Mode
(plagal *protus*, later Hypodorian)

Third Mode
(authentic *deuterus*, later Phrygian)

Fourth Mode
(plagal *deuterus*, later Hypophrygian)

Fifth Mode
(authentic *tritus*, later Lydian)

Sixth Mode
(plagal *tritus*, later Hypolydian)

Seventh Mode
(authentic *tetrardus*, later Mixolydian)

Eighth Mode
(plagal *tetrardus*, later Hypomixolydian)

These eight scales, which were originally only designated with their numbers within the system, apparently in the ninth or tenth century received names borrowed from the ancient Greek scales, but now applied in a different way. That is, while in the middle ages the succession, Dorian-Phrygian-Lydian-Mixolydian, through the respective beginning tones, represented four tonal series beginning with D and going upward, the same succession in ancient Greek times referred to a series beginning with E and then descending:

A certain principle operates here even if it is erroneous; when and how this error crept in must for the time being remain unanswered. Some evidence perhaps justifies the assumption that the confusion arose in the

ninth or tenth century and that it can be explained as a mistaken transference of the names of the Greek "transposition scales" to the Gregorian
modes.[1]   Yet it remains open to question whether the change may not
have occurred still earlier in Asia Minor or Byzantium.[2]

Merely to cite the range of the ecclesiastical modes helps little.   It must
be clearly understood that scale and mode are two very different things:
mode is living music; but the scale is only a dead abstraction, the material
of the mode arranged according to pitch.   Just as one could scarcely
explain the playing of chess by merely arranging the pieces in order,
so one could scarcely define the notion of mode by means of such a lifeless
abstraction as the scale.   Scales are merely collections of material from
which a given mode takes the tones it needs for its particular purposes.
So, for example, from the twelve-tone chromatic scale into which we
ordinarily divide the octave, we select the tones with which our major
and minor modes deal.   Whereas the scale is, as we know, an abstraction,
the mode is something living, and therefore its meaning is hard to grasp
—it can never be defined.   One could define it as a sum of melodic or
harmonic motive-impulses attached to certain tones and to a certain
extent tending toward the principal tone or final.   The way certain tones

---

[1] Besides the actual (original) modes, the Greeks had a system of so-called transposition scales
so constructed that the original scales were all transposed within the octave E–E and the resulting eight-tone series were so supplemented that they were expanded into forms identical with
our pure minor scales extending through two octaves:

As may be seen, Dorian-Phrygian-Lydian-Mixolydian here refer, as in the ecclesiastical modes,
to a set of four tonal series ascending by degrees even though beginning on another initial tone.

[2] Compare Peter Wagner, *Elemente des Gregorianischen Gesanges*. Regensburg, Kösel–Pustet,
1917.   Page 111.

are emphasized while others are subordinated chiefly determines the mode.

Certain relations in Gregorian music are preëminently suited to illustrate the difference between scale and mode. Here, for example the first (Dorian) and the eighth (Hypomixolydian) scales have the same range in that both go from D to D, and they therefore use exactly the same tonal materials. The fact that one can nevertheless easily decide whether a melody is in one or the other of the two modes depends, among other things, upon the circumstance that in the Dorian mode D and A are the tones most plainly emphasized, whereas in the Hypomixolydian mode G and C are preferred. An equally interesting example of such a conflict between scale and mode may be observed in the second (Hypodorian) mode. The scale of this mode extends from A to A, but while the scale thus has B as its second tone, the mode almost always avoids this tone. The situation is similar in the Hypophrygian mode, with a range from B to B, where, although B is the lowest tone, melodies in this mode almost never make use of it. Mode and scale are, therefore, by no means identical, and if one wishes to learn more of the nature of the Gregorian modes he must not stop with the tones, but must come to understand the melodic laws which govern their use. Most important here is the question of the basic pillars of melodies and, therefore, of modes: tonic (principal tone, which could perhaps also be called "tone of resolution"), and dominant (which might be designated as the "suspense tone" or "tone of tension").

It is generally known that these two concepts are inextricably connected not merely with the Gregorian chant but with the idea of "modes" in general. If we hear a melody we are inclined to look for the keynote—the tone upon which the melody seems to rest—among the lower tones; we involuntarily pay less attention to the higher tones. The reason for this is surely that we associate with the term keynote the feeling of rest, of resolution. It seems almost unthinkable to us that a melody should end otherwise than on the tonic or on the tonic triad; otherwise we should miss the feeling of completion. This fact depends in part upon the tradition gradually established that the tonic close has the effect of a conventional signal to announce with unmistakable clearness that the music has come to an end. The conception of music as a sort of unfolding of energy doubtless lies at the root of the origin of such a tradition, an unfolding which starts out from rest and returns to it again, bringing the composition to a close in a natural way. Now, it so happens that we associate the feeling of increasing energy with an ascending series of tones, just as, in general, we get more of an impression of tension from higher tones than from lower tones, a fact that probably depends upon natural physiological causes. The normal relaxation of the vocal chords at the close of a spoken sentence quite mechanically produces a falling of the voice. It is natural and easy to explain, therefore, that the dominant —the tone about which the tension of the melody is centered—should lie above the tonic, the tone of resolution, both in the ecclesiastical modes and in major and minor. But there is this difference between the modern and the medieval modes: that the modern are characterized by a constant relation in which the dominant is always a fifth above the principle tone, while the medieval are much freer and more varied in this respect.

Evidence of this fact is found in the psalm melodies (certain short, recitative-like Gregorian melodic formulas), which are used in the performance of the verses of the psalms with the doxology in the introit (the first part of the music in the Catholic mass). Since the introit melodies occur in all eight Gregorian modes and the verse of the psalm associated with them naturally must use the mode of their introit, there is an intonation of this kind for every mode. In the first mode it is as follows (here cited only with the text of the doxology):

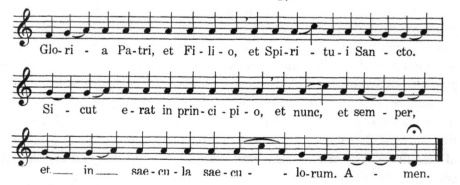

Glo-ri - a Pa-tri, et Fi - li - o, et Spi-ri - tu-i San - cto.

Si - cut e - rat in prin-ci - pi - o, et nunc, et sem - per,

et.____ in ____ sae - cu - la sae - cu - - lo-rum. A - men.

The final (which in Gregorian melodies is as a rule identical with the tonic) is here, as can be seen, D. The tone around which the melody develops its "state of tension" is A, the dominant of the first mode. In the example given, the interval between the tonic and the dominant is, therefore, the same as in the modern modes: namely, a fifth.

Passing on to the second mode, however, this relation changes:

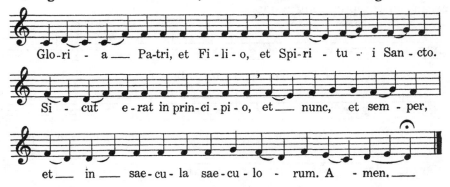

Glo-ri - a — Pa-tri, et Fi-li-o, et Spi-ri - tu - i San - cto.

Si - cut e-rat in prin-ci-pi-o, et — nunc, et sem - per,

et — in — sae-cu-la sae-cu-lo - rum. A - men. —

As in the first mode, the D is the principal tone. Note that the plagal mode, as I have said, always has the same tonic as the corresponding authentic mode. The dominant, however, is no longer A, but F, and the interval between the tonic and dominant is thus a third.

In the third mode:

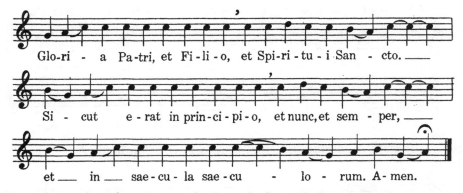

Glo-ri - a Pa-tri, et Fi-li-o, et Spi-ri-tu-i San - cto. —

Si - cut e-rat in prin-ci-pi-o, et nunc, et sem - per, —

et — in — sae-cu-la sae-cu - lo - rum. A- men.

E is the tonic (the piece ends irregularly, as occasionally happens in melodies of a more recitative character). The dominant is not B, as we might expect, but C.

Originally B was actually a dominant; later—presumably about the year 1000—the dominant function was transferred to C, apparently because by that time musicians had become more sensitive to the dominant relation B–F (diminished fifth, augmented fourth) and consequently did not wish to accept, for such an important place as the dominant, a tone that might so easily produce a dissonance.

In the fourth mode, E is the tonic and A the dominant. Originally

G was the dominant of this mode; but it was changed at the same time
as that of the preceding mode:

F is the tonic of the fifth mode (the intonation closes here irregularly
on A); the dominant is C:

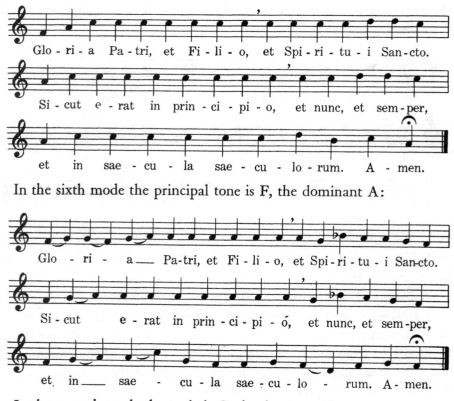

In the seventh mode the tonic is G, the dominant D:

Glo - ri - a Pa-tri, et Fi-li-o, et Spi-ri - tu - i San - cto.

Si - cut — e-rat in prin-ci-pi-o, et nunc, et sem - per,

et — in — sae-cu-la sae-cu - lo-rum. A - men.

In the eighth mode the tonic is G, the dominant C. As in the third mode, the dominant here was originally B, but it was changed to C at the same time as the dominant of the Phrygian mode and for the same reasons:

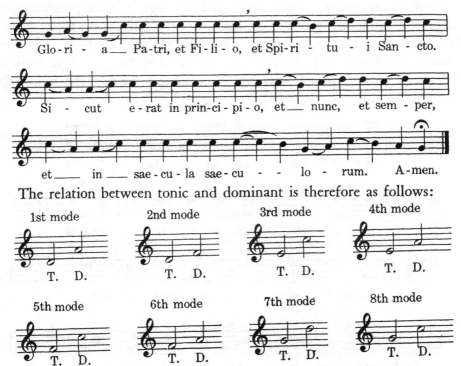

Glo-ri - a — Pa-tri, et Fi-li - o, et Spi-ri - tu - i San - cto.

Si - cut e-rat in prin-ci-pi-o, et — nunc, et sem - per,

et — in — sae-cu-la sae-cu - - lo - rum. A-men.

The relation between tonic and dominant is therefore as follows:

1st mode   2nd mode   3rd mode   4th mode

T. D.   T. D.   T. D.   T. D.

5th mode   6th mode   7th mode   8th mode

T. D.   T. D.   T. D.   T. D.

As an aid to memory, the following rule may be formulated (it must always be thought of as merely a rule, as it has nothing to do with the origin of the practice): (1) In the authentic modes the dominant is a fifth above the tonic; the B, however, is not used as a dominant but is replaced by the C. (2) In the plagal modes the dominant is a third below the dominant of the corresponding authentic mode; and here, too, B as a dominant is replaced by C.

In addition to the relation between tonic and dominant, a certain element of "pentatonic" musical feeling is also characteristic of the Gregorian modes. By "pentatonic" music is meant, of course, the musical style associated with the pentatonic (five-tone) scale. This succession of tones, which is characteristic of primitive music, seems consciously to avoid the half-tone step. It occurs in two forms, and each series can make use of any one of its five tones for a beginning tone as desired:

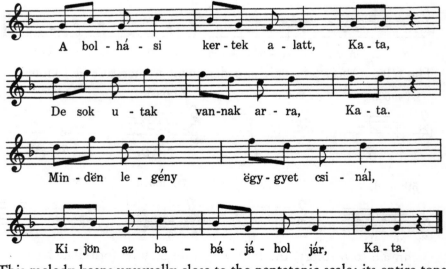

In this scale we can recognize the tonal language of exotic peoples, especially the music of the Far East; but European folk music, for example that of Scotland and the contemporary folk melodies of the Hungarians and the Russian-Tartars, is strikingly influenced by this particular musical idea. As an example of such a pure pentatonic melody, the following Hungarian song may be taken: [3]

A bol - há - si   ker - tek   a - latt,   Ka - ta,

De sok   u - tak   van-nak   ar - ra,   Ka - ta.

Min - dën   le - gény   ëgy - gyet   csi - nál,

Ki - jön   az   ba - bá - já - hol   jár,   Ka - ta.

This melody keeps unusually close to the pentatonic scale; its entire tonal material consists of:

---

[3] See Kodály, Zoltán: *A Magyar Népzene.* Budapest, Egyetemi nyomda, 1937, p. 32.

Without being really pentatonic, the Gregorian chant is marked by a high degree of pentatonic feeling; the pentatonic idea, the original source of the "homophonic" ecclesiastical modes, is not to be denied. Likewise in medieval folk songs we find traces of the strong and pure linear treatment, which is characteristic of this type of music.[4]

Although the tonic-dominant relation combined with a certain shyness about using the half-step progression (the E–F and B–C progressions are avoided as much as possible) is characteristic of the ecclesiastical modes, certain other particular melodic motives so characteristic that they almost have the power of determining the mode can be found.   In the first mode we find, for example, the distinctive idiom:

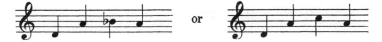

The following progression is typical of the third mode:

and the fifth mode makes considerable use of the following figure:

---

[4] In modern music too, a certain tendency toward the pentatonic can be observed.   The entire history of music could justifiably be written as the *History of the Leading-Tone Step:* how this effect was found originally in certain Gregorian modes; how in the beginning it was carefully avoided until gradually musicians learned to appreciate it and introduced it in modes to which it was foreign; and how, with the transition to polyphony, it then took an established form in the dominant-tonic cadence and finally led to the whole Wagnerian and Post-Wagnerian chromaticism.

In our contemporary music pentatonic usages may be clearly perceived, as, for example, in pieces of modern French, Russian, and Hungarian music entirely independent of each other, as well as in the work of Nordic composers such as Sibelius and especially Carl Nielsen. This similarity between older and more modern music, however, depends only to a slight extent upon a direct connection.   Historically, the actual circumstance is apparently that the evolution had reached a point at which two movements separate, namely, a trend toward the dominant seventh chord and a movement in an opposite direction.   The latter is most characteristic in modern music and—whether through pentatonic practice or atonality—constitutes an entirely comprehensible counteraction to the usually strong emphasis on the cadence customary in the eighteenth and nineteenth centuries.

In these formulas (and for that matter in many others, about which I cannot go into detail here) the tonic generally has such a clear-cut and definitive effect that the mode can be determined easily and the final, because of this, sounds convincing. Yet it sometimes happens in Gregorian melodies that the final stands in an arbitrary relation to these formulas which are typical of the particular mode. If we hear, for example, the figure cited as characteristic of the first mode, we are immediately inclined to regard it in terms of this mode, and, as a rule, the D will be the final. But occasionally we may be deceived. As an example I should like to cite the Kyrie melody, *"Fons bonitatis."* It is in the third mode and has E as the principal tone. It begins:

The figure D–A–C obviously plays a prominent rôle here, and one involuntarily expects the melody to end on D; but in spite of all expectations it actually closes with an E. Another interesting case is the Offertorium *Invocavit,* which is actually in the sixth mode and consequently has F as principal tone, but which nevertheless begins in true Dorian fashion:

only to end, otherwise quite correctly, according to the usual convention of the sixth mode.

This and similar cases are often found in Gregorian melodies. This fact leads to the conclusion that there was still a good way to go before the domination of the tonic should completely penetrate the style.

Simultaneously with the transition from the Gregorian homophony to the polyphony of the middle ages, a decisive change gradually took place in the history of the ecclesiastical modes. The Gregorian modes (which one might define as a sum of melodic characteristics) apparently passed over into the new art, so far as the form is concerned. But from now on they were subjected to the growing demands of the opposing viewpoint, that of harmony, and were thereby forced into a subordinate position and finally ended in the major and minor forms which are essentially based upon chords. The ecclesiastical modes of polyphony are the transition form between the Gregorian modes and the major-minor system. Although harmonic considerations already begin to play a strong rôle, nevertheless the melodic viewpoint is still quite noticeable, so that a definition of these "polyphonic" modes is possible only if both harmonic and melodic factors are taken into consideration.

In the transition to polyphony, the chief modification in the ecclesiastical modes was the introduction of the leading-tone cadence (the half-tone step between the seventh and eighth degrees) in almost all modes.[5] Although the Gregorian modes used the flat (the use of which will be discussed in detail later) only as a sign of alteration, nevertheless some of these modes (the fifth and sixth) had a half-tone step below the principal tone and thus the possibility of leading-tone cadences. But appreciation of this effect, which we call the full close, came only with polyphonic music; henceforth it was felt that such cadences as the following did not have a convincing effect:

whereas raising the third of the A minor triad resulted in a much stronger and more convincing cadence. Soon, therefore, the use of the major third in the dominant triad became the rule, and indeed in modes, too, in which the particular tone was originally not available. To this end different chromatic signs for raising a tone were introduced that were foreign to the Gregorian modes. The C in the Dorian mode was changed to C-sharp, and similarly in the Mixolydian the F was changed to F-sharp; in the Aeolian mode (to which we shall refer again later) the seventh step was raised from G to G-sharp. In the Phrygian mode, on the other

---

[5] Another important change might also be mentioned here: that the melodic dominant, which stood in a changing interval relationship to the tonic in the different Gregorian modes, is uniformly fixed on the fifth degree of the scale (calculated from the tonic) in the "polyphonic" ecclesiastical modes.

hand, the D was retained; the D-sharp was in general used only in very
exceptional cases.   Moreover the tonic triad with minor third was seldom
used as a closing chord (often the third of the final chord was omitted).
This led to the raising of the F to F-sharp in the Dorian mode; in the
Phrygian the G was changed to G-sharp, and in the Aeolian C to C-sharp.
Finally, just as in the case of the Gregorian chant, in descending progressions or in figures which turned back from B, B-flat was often used
in all modes instead of B.   If, however, the progressions continued upward
to the C, the B was not lowered.   And where it was necessary to avoid
dissonant intervals such as F–B, the B-flat was introduced.   When the
F had a tendency to go to the G, F was often changed to F-sharp.   To
illustrate these chromatic alterations as well as the ecclesiastical modes in
general, let us introduce at this point several cadence structures.   I give
them exclusively in authentic modes, since in polyphonic style the difference between plagal and authentic modes—although still maintained
by theorists—caused no particular modifications in the treatment.

The following example is from the end of the motet *Adoramus te
Christe*.   Notice the flat in the third measure from the end.   Palestrina
introduced it doubtless because of the descending progression.   In the
same measure the editor [6] has likewise introduced a flat above the last note
of the bass.   A usually valid rule states that when the upper auxiliary is

Dorian   Palestrina

---

[6] The motet appears in the complete edition of the works of Palestrina (Leipzig, Breitkopf und
Härtel), Vol. 5, pp. 176 f.   This particular volume is edited by Franz Espagne.

used, the minor second should be employed if possible. This rule was so well known that the composers often did not write in the flat at all but assumed that the singer would introduce it himself. In the tenor, we have in the third from the last and in the next to the last bar the raising of the seventh degree C to C-sharp, and in the final bar the F in the alto is raised for the sake of the major third in the final chord.

From the motet *Domine, non sum dignus*

In this mode the use of the flat is less common than in the "homophonic" Phrygian, where it is frequent. The third in the final chord is raised, and this change makes the raising of the F necessary because other-

wise there would be an augmented second. In the Phrygian mode we
frequently find the following cadence, too:

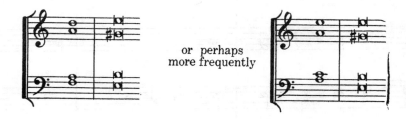

or perhaps
more frequently

The Lydian mode really exists only in the homophonic ecclesiastical
modes. As soon as we go into polyphony, the lack of a consonant triad
on the fourth degree becomes too noticeable, and the B is changed to
B-flat in order to provide for a major triad on the subdominant. By
this the mode is changed into F Ionian; with the B-flat constantly used
it is like a transposed C major scale. It is significant that in the polyphonic treatment of the *Magnificat* (the *Canticum B. Mariae Virginis*,
Luke I, 46–55, written in the eight ecclesiastical modes after the eight
modes of the Psalms) Palestrina allows the fifth mode to cadence on A
—in the Gregorian example the A is the final—and in the sixth mode
he uses the B-flat, which also avoids the Lydian form.

From the motet Lapidabant Stephanum

Palestrina here first makes a full close (measures 2–3—although the feeling of complete finality is avoided through the use of what we now call the "deceptive cadence"), which is later followed by a cadence: IV–I (a "plagal cadence," as it was called in the nineteenth century). This type of cadence structure is commonly used in all modes.

The frequent use of the flat is striking in the Mixolydian, for by this means the mode at times gets into a remarkable situation hovering between major and minor, as in the closing measures of the *Benedictus* from Palestrina's mass *Dies sanctificatus:*

The reduction in the number of the ecclesiastical modes produced by the fusion of the authentic and plagal scales was offset in polyphony by the addition of two new modes, the Aeolian and the Ionian, which are not included in the official Gregorian theory. Although practical musicians had long used both of these modes, they were nevertheless not recognized in theory until the sixteenth century. The first one to advocate their adoption in the legitimate family of modes was the Swiss theorist, Glareanus, who in his famous work *Dodecachordon,* published in 1547, seeks to prove that the theorists ought to consider twelve modes instead of eight, as they formerly did. To the eight Gregorian modes he added namely the following:

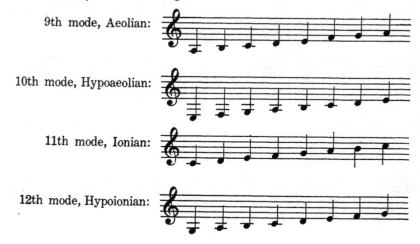

These modes, whose authentic and plagal forms also fuse in actual practice, play an important rôle, especially in the polyphonic music of the sixteenth century. Indeed, by their transition into the major and minor (which they resembled greatly from the beginning) they gradually superseded the earlier modes. The following is an example of an Aeolian cadence:

From the motet *Hic est vere martyr*

The flat can be used in the Aeolian, but it is hardly as common here as it is, for example, in the Dorian.

From the mass *Ave Regina coelorum*

Ionian

Palestrina

The Ionian mode uses the flat frequently and in a characteristic manner, as in the example below and on the facing page (from another place in the same mass).

In summary, we have learned that the polyphony of the sixteenth century made use of only five modes (the Lydian passes over into Ionian, as I have said): Dorian, Phrygian, Mixolydian, Aeolian, Ionian.

These original modes could be transposed, however, a fourth higher

by the use of a flat (the only fixed signature that was normally used). By this means the following scales are obtained:

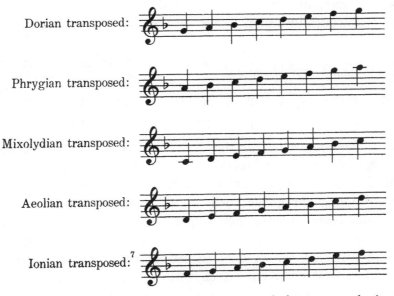

These transpositions were used with unusual frequency during the sixteenth century in order to bring compositions into a more pleasing and singable register.

---

[7] Note that E-flat in the transposed modes corresponds to B-flat in the non-transposed scales, but that it was ordinarily used only to supplement the flat in the signature, and hence not in original scales.

To understand the essential difference between the "polyphonic" ecclesiastical modes and major or minor, one should study the problem of
the leading tone. A modern ear, accustomed to hearing a half step
between the seventh and eighth degrees of the scale, feels a peculiar
charm in the fact that the ecclesiastical modes do not use one single
definite interval at this place, but use sometimes a whole and sometimes
a half step. Likewise the free use of the B-flat for melodic reasons and
the raising of the third of certain definite triads, which occurs with equal
freedom, produce harmonic variations which sound refreshing and
strange. Every ecclesiastical mode actually has at its disposal many more
chordal possibilities than the major and minor scales. If we compare,
for example, the Dorian with D minor (the two having almost the same
scale) we see that the Dorian has two triads (D major and D minor)
on the first degree, whereas the D minor scale has only one. On the
second degree there are two possibilities available for the ecclesiastical
mode, but only one for the D minor scale.

The following illustration shows the resources ordinarily available:

Dorian: I   I   II   II⁰ III IΙΙ̶ IV   IV   V   V   VI   VI⁰ VII VII⁰

D minor: I   II⁰ IΙΙ̶   IV   V   VI   VII⁰

As may be seen, we have in the Dorian no less than six pure triads—the
most valuable tonal combinations—which deviate from D minor: D
major, E minor, F major, G major, A minor, and C major.

In addition to the greater richness which the particular ecclesiastical
modes thus possess within their respective fields, they have the greater
number of modes. While modern music has only two modes, major
and minor (modes which may, indeed, be transposed to every degree
of the chromatic scale, but which maintain the same arrangement of
intervals), the former polyphony may employ, as has been said, no less
than five modes, each of which has its own pronounced individuality.

If modern music is inferior to the older style in this respect, it is nevertheless greatly superior in the matter of modulatory resources. Perhaps

_____

[8] The diminished and augmented triads can be used only as chords of the sixth in the Palestrina style. This will be discussed later.

it is a question whether, in connection with the ecclesiastical modes, one can speak of modulation at all in the real sense of the term. At any rate, change of signature is quite unknown here (because one never passes over from a transposed to an untransposed mode, or vice versa). Thus intentional contrast between the transpositions of the modes, upon which modern music depends for one of its most important effects, is entirely foreign to the ecclesiastical system. And yet a certain striving for variation can be observed here as well. Since it would naturally be tiresome and inartistic to have the same cadence constantly returning in a composition, provision is made for as many different cadences as possible to be used. This provision, however, really only corresponds to the "transitions," as in modern music one calls attempts to enliven the feeling of tonality by slight incursions into the territory of other keys— procedures which have no lasting influence and which do not introduce genuine modulation (that is, the transference of the tonic feeling to new chords).

Each of the "polyphonic" ecclesiastical modes (and this is also true of the "homophonic" modes) reveals its tendency toward this sort of transient modulation in its individual way. Theoretically, one can indeed cadence on any desired step of the scales (and to this end the traditional accidentals may be used). But the individual character of each particular mode depends largely upon what cadences it favors or avoids. Thus, for example, the Dorian, apart from the tonic cadences, closes most frequently on the dominant, A (A: V–i or V–I). In this mode, on the other hand, the subdominant plays a relatively modest rôle; cadences on the third degree, F (mediant-mode), are preferred. The cadence on C (Ionian) is less common, while E (Phrygian) is rarely used.

In the Phrygian next to the E, the A (Aeolian) is preferred as a cadence tone; but cadences on G (Mixolydian) are very much favored. In addition, cadences on D (Dorian with or without F-sharp) and C (Ionian) are used quite often, whereas the F is rarely selected for a closing tone. In the Mixolydian mode after the G, the D (Dorian, with or without F-sharp), and C (Ionian) are the most favored cadence tones; A is likewise quite common, but F and E are used much less often.

In the Aeolian the subdominant D (Dorian) is obviously preferred to the dominant E as a closing tone (cadences on E in general play a strikingly unimportant rôle). In addition, C, G, and F are used. The

Ionian mode uses its dominant G most of all next to the C; A and D likewise appear quite often, while E and F are more unusual:

	Common Cadences	Less Common	Rare
Dorian	D, A, F	G, C	E
Phrygian	E, A, G	D, C	F
Mixolydian	G, D, C	A	F, E
Aeolian	A, D, C	G, F	E
Ionian	C, G, A	D	F, E

From the table we see that in their relationship to each other, the "polyphonic" ecclesiastical modes follow neither the Gregorian music nor the major and minor system, but exclusively their own special procedures. We would expect the C, the dominant of the Gregorian Phrygian mode, to play one of the chief rôles as a cadence tone in the polyphonic Phrygian; nevertheless the A is preferred. If on the other hand we look at the modes from the major-minor viewpoint and consequently think that the tonic, dominant, subdominant, and relative tonalities must constitute their chief harmonic supports, we will also be disappointed. In the Dorian and Ionian modes, for example, the subdominant by no means attains the expected significance; in the Phrygian and Aeolian the dominant falls surprisingly into the background, and in the Mixolydian the mediant mode is not so important as might be expected.

As a general rule for all the ecclesiastical modes, we can say that, next to the tonic, the dominant (fifth above the tonic) is the most important cadence tone. Only where the dominant chord must fall on B (which drops out of consideration entirely because of the lack of a usable, consonant fifth) does the subdominant come into prominence as a substitute. Otherwise the subdominant plays for the most part a much less important rôle than in the more modern scales; however, the position of the relative mode is, as a rule, quite significant.

One characteristic of the ecclesiastical modes is, briefly, that they have greater variety but less logic than the modern modes. The illogicality found in this aspect of medieval music, as in many other aspects, is felt today as a peculiar charm, as the expression of a pleasant, unaffected naturalness, of a refreshing, unrestrained musical feeling, and as a happy contrast to that which, in later times, is often an unattractive and pedantically exact schematization.

MELODY

The polyphony of the Palestrina style rests essentially upon simultaneously sounding melodic lines; its basis is melodies.

These melodies differ in many respects from the concepts associated in more modern times (eighteenth and nineteenth centuries) with the word *melody*. In the first place the treatment of intervals is much simpler and stricter. All chromaticisms and all dissonant skips are avoided, and the attitude toward the rhythmic-metrical problem is proportionately less one-sided. The Palestrina music moves in free, prose-like rhythms in contrast to the poetic, strict rhythmic pattern of the eighteenth and nineteenth centuries (especially that of the Vienna classicism) with its accurately measured symmetry (the constructive material consists chiefly of groups of from two to four measures) which, if carried to extremes, can be unbearably conventional and limited.

The linear treatment of the Palestrina music reveals a marked inner coherence and an understanding of what is, in the truest sense, organic, which is indeed sought after in every style species. It abhors the rough and inelegant and rejoices in the free and natural. It avoids strong, unduly sharp accents and extreme contrasts of every kind and expresses itself always in a characteristically smooth and pleasing manner that may seem at first somewhat uniform and unimposing but that soon reveals the richly shaded expression of a superior culture.

According to a famous Italian Renaissance architect, Leone Battista Alberti, "Beauty is a sort of chordal combination, a harmony between the different units which does not allow anything to be added or taken away without having an injurious effect upon the whole." This definition applies also to the Palestrina music, in which the constructive sense is strongly influenced by the viewpoints of the late Renaissance. In contrast to the often somewhat fantastically diffuse style of the middle ages, the Palestrina style rested on the principle: not a single note too many or too few. All details must unite in entirely undisturbed harmony, must fuse into a higher unity in spite of individual independence. An absolute, completely free balance between the elements was required; no one element could be emphasized at the expense of another; everything must work together smoothly and harmoniously. Let us examine one

of the melodies of Palestrina: the beginning of the upper part from his
five-part offertorium *Ave Maria:*

A - ve - Ma - ri - a, a - - - ve Ma - - - - -

ri - - - - - - - - - - a, a - - - -

- - - ve Ma - - - ri - - - - - a,

The text consists of *"Ave Maria"* repeated three times. The melody,
which is fifteen measures in length, is closely knit into a continuous whole
from beginning to end. Figuratively speaking, it is impossible to insert
even so much as the point of a knife between any two notes; one note
follows the other in an unbroken, organic unity. There is no trace of
exact symmetrical phrase structure; 2¾ measures are used for the first
third of the text, 5¾ for the second, and 6½ for the last.

Genuine sequences do not occur. In general, Palestrina uses them only
rarely (mostly in earlier works), since the balance of the linear treatment
can easily be displaced by the overemphasis which they place upon a
particular motive.[1]

The line of the *Ave Maria* melody forms a curve which begins relatively high on E, moves downward to the A, and then rises again to the E,
after which it touches upon the F and descends gradually. In bar 7
it takes another turn upward, reaches its lowest point (F) in bar 8, then
ascends somewhat abruptly to the culmination point G (bar 11) and
finally glides downward after a small opposing curve (bars 12–13) to

---

[1] The following sequences, however, are exceptions which are frequently found in works of
the best composers of the sixteenth century generally:

and

The parallel construction of measures 4 to 5 of this melody is related to the last example. It
must not be considered a genuine sequence, however, but as a scalewise spinning-out of the figure.

the closing tone A. Obviously the melody is treated throughout in a masterful and even fashion; ascending and descending movements are balanced according to Palestrina's usual practice. Bach, on the other hand, prefers to begin low and slowly work upward with a steadily increasing tension to a point of culmination and, when this is reached, to descend to the cadence suddenly, almost explosively. Here the ascent is by far the most interesting and most broadly developed part. The contrast to this type of curve, which is so characteristic of Bach, is frequently found in the Gregorian chant where the melody rises quickly and lightly and then glides down again in broad circles like a bird, floating slowly with almost imperceptible movement. The melodic form of the Palestrina time is an intermediate type between these two extremes, entirely in accordance with the constant striving toward balance and harmonic rest characteristic of this style.

Note in the melody above that stepwise progression predominates. Of the larger intervals we find only the fifth (both ascending and descending) at the beginning and the ascending skip of the fourth in bar 9; otherwise there are only ascending and descending skips of the third. This preference for conjunct motion is most characteristic of the Palestrina melody (as it is of the Gregorian chant). But a melody which proceeded exclusively in small seconds and thirds would eventually produce a dull, soporific effect; it would be an absurdity. While the Gregorian chant ordinarily uses large and small seconds and thirds, pure fourths and fifths, the Palestrina style normally uses the following intervals, as we have already seen:

Ascending and Descending					Ascending only
Major and minor second.	Major and minor third.	Perfect fourth.	Perfect fifth.	Perfect octave.	Minor sixth.

We see, therefore, that augmented and diminished intervals are excluded; as a rule the major sixth is likewise avoided, and sevenths and all intervals greater than the octave are not considered at all. Likewise foreign to the style is the chromatic half-tone step (the minor second step which arises from the progression from a tone to its chromatic alteration, as C to C-sharp or B to B-flat). Furthermore, we see that the larger intervals are subject to very particular treatment in that they are compensated by stepwise progression. The skip of the fifth at the beginning of the melody, for example, is filled out in the following measures, as is the skip of the fourth in measure 9 (although somewhat later), and so on. It is thus normal in the Palestrina style that skips are compensated by stepwise progressions or—as is also somewhat common—by skips in the opposite direction. But it often happens, too, that stepwise movement and skips in the same direction alternate (whether the skip comes before or after the stepwise progression), or that a skip is followed by another skip in the same direction. The limits are made too narrow if, as in some counterpoint books, the succession of two skips in the same direction is entirely forbidden (except where the skips occur in quarters—that is, in note values that are one-half the unit of measure). The practice of the Palestrina style is more accurately defined by the following rules:

1. In ascending movement it is better to have the larger intervals at the beginning of the curve; the large skip should therefore precede the smaller as in the opening theme of Palestrina's four-part motet *Ad te levavi:* [2]

or in his motet *Surge propera:*

2. In descending motion, on the other hand, the smaller intervals generally precede the larger, as in the following measures from Palestrina's offertorium *Dextera Domini:*

If the progressions occur in greater note values (in whole notes and in halves, when the half is the unit of measure) these rules must be considered tendencies which must not be disregarded but which under certain circumstances must give way to more important considerations.

---

[2] Here we have a suggestion of tone painting. The words mean: "To Thee I raise mine eyes."

But if a movement continues in quarters (halves of the units of measure), then the rules are carefully observed. Indeed this is true not only with regard to the succession of intervals; all melodic laws of the Palestrina style are most strictly observed in the use of quarters (because here the melodic connection is keenly felt, whereas increasing note values tend to weaken this feeling).

Another of the chief melodic laws of the Palestrina style warns against ascending skips from accented notes. In the stricter sense, this law applies only to quarters; it does not apply at all to whole notes, and even in progressions in half notes the law is frequently broken, although there is undeniably a tendency to observe the law. In quarters the law is fully valid.[3] Thus while the following idiom is most common in Palestrina melodies: (music) its inversion: (music)

is so rare that one must consider it foreign to the style. If we wish, therefore, to remain within the norms of the style, we must avoid the ascending skip from the accented quarter, though descending skips from accented quarters are entirely correct. The following ornaments, all of which are common in Palestrina's works, will confirm what I have said:

---

[3] See *The Style of Palestrina and the Dissonance*, pp. 54 ff. and my article: "Das 'Sprunggesetz' des Palestrina-Stils bei betonten Viertelnoten (halben Taktzeiten)," *Bericht über den musikwissenschaftlichen Kongress in Basel 1924*, pp. 211 ff. Leipzig: Breitkopf und Härtel, 1925.

But it is quite permissible to skip upwards from unaccented quarters, as may be seen from many of the examples above; and the descending skip is also possible:

From the foregoing it will be seen that decided differences exist between the treatment of the intervals in the Palestrina style and in the Gregorian song. For example, while the Gregorian chant abounds in pentatonic figures such as the following:

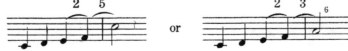

the Palestrina style avoids such figures because the succession of intervals is contrary to its basic principles. We can easily understand why an idiom of this kind: 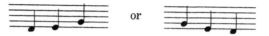 (the *cambiata,* an extremely well-liked device) was preferred to this: and why the inversion of the *cambiata,* although permissible in longer note values, is not written in quarters: . Equally enlightening is the fact that figures such as the following are avoided:

---

[4] This idiom is rare in the Palestrina style.

[5] Likewise very rare.

[6] This follows, of course, from the rule mentioned above. The theory of the seventeenth century (which clearly perceived this relation, whereas the eighteenth and nineteenth centuries lost sight of it) motivated its restriction with the statement that it is always best if stepwise progressions are continued on to an accented half note. Compare, for example, the citation from Andreas Lorentes: *El Porque de la musica* (Alçala, 1672) in *The Style of Palestrina,* p. 67.

The figure  is, on the contrary, usable only
if the lowest tone is followed by the second above. (If the second below
is written, the larger interval precedes the smaller in descending motion.) Larger skips than the third are nevertheless not permissible
under similar circumstances, even if the intervals are correctly arranged.
Examples such as the following:

are accordingly contrary to the style. Nor can two or more skips in the
same direction come in succession when the movement is in quarters, as
for example:

On the other hand two skips may well come in succession if they are in
opposite directions even in quarter-note movement. The following
cadence figure is one of the favorite devices (and rightly so, because it is
unusually well balanced):

Ascending skips which follow quarter-note movement descending by
step are generally usable but produce the best effect if the skip is made
to an unaccented half or to a relatively accented quarter note after not

more than three successive quarters: Conse-

quently the following is not so good:

In such cases as the foregoing, it is best to skip to a half note which is tied
over:

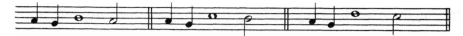

Such figures, which are most usable when the ascending skip occurs after a quarter introduced by step from above, are most rare in the inversion, that is, if the quarter note is introduced stepwise from below

and the succeeding skip is downward. Devices such as

are nevertheless fairly common (although not nearly so common as the

inversion) while  or  is prac-

tically excluded.

In the music of Palestrina in general, a striking difference is found in the treatment of the ascending and descending intervals. It is evident here that ascending skips are much more carefully compensated for or filled out than descending skips. While figures such as:

occur rather often in half notes, much less often do we find inversions of them, such as:

Similarly a larger skip downward is often followed by another skip (in the opposite direction, of course). On the other hand, a large skip upward is almost always followed by a descending stepwise progression. This must be so because the tone to which one skips in the first case is the "low tone" and the other is the "high tone," and because ascending skips attract the listener's attention more than descending ones. Therefore care is always taken that the former are softened by effects less energetic in character (since the whole might otherwise easily sound too restless and active). Descending skips have, on the other hand, a less pronounced effect and therefore do not require compensation by being followed by particularly smooth progressions.

In quarters the stepwise, or, more accurately, the stepwise-passing kind

of movement, is by far the most common. But in stepwise movement
one sometimes "turns" and comes back to the same tone, for example:

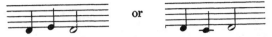

These two figures are equally usable if, as in the present example, they
return to a half note. But if the note to which one returns from the
upper or lower second is a quarter, then there is a difference: for while

the turning on the lower second: is very common,

the inversion is most rare in the Palestrina style.

Apparently the identity of the first and third quarters in the figure with
the upper auxiliary was felt to be too inexpressive. Berardi expresses this
in the viewpoint of the seventeenth century, which is more chord-
conscious, as follows: "Moreover the figure called *girandoletta* or *gioco* is
forbidden, particularly where the cantus firmus remains over the same
chord":[7]

[7] *Miscellanea musicale* (Bologna, 1689), p. 136. Compare further Berardi: *Il perchè musicale*
(Bologna, 1693), p. 32: "The reason the *girandoletta* or *gioco* is prohibited, especially when
the cantus firmus does not move, is that one hears two octaves or two fifths repeated over the
same chord; moreover in quarter-note passages one should use the figure called the *conducimento*,
which is a stepwise movement from low to high and from high to low. . . ."

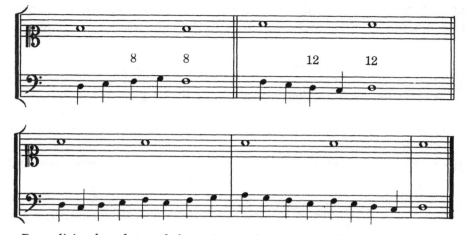

Berardi is, therefore, of the opinion that such auxiliary figures should be strictly forbidden, especially where the position of the other part produces the return not only to the same tone but above all to the same chord. But if we compare the practice of the sixteenth century with the rules of Berardi, we soon find that he makes too broad a generalization. He does not distinguish at all between figures employing the upper second and those using the lower second as the auxiliary note. As I have said, this distinction existed nevertheless, doubtless because particular care and attention were involuntarily given to the continuation from the upper auxiliary, which is very strongly emphasized by its position. Consequently the upper auxiliary is not used very much, especially when rhythmic identity is added to melodic identity, because the triviality of the effect thereby becomes so much more striking. Thus, as has been said, one should be able to use the upper auxiliary before either a half note or a still longer note value, but not before another quarter note. (This rule is valid regardless of whether the upper auxiliary is on the second or the fourth quarter.) Such figures as the following occur relatively often:

The following device, on the other hand, is so rare with Palestrina that it can be called unusable:

Nevertheless, its inversion is common:

Likewise figures like the following can be found in Palestrina, though

they are rare: , while the inversion was most rare

even in composers of the earlier part of the sixteenth century and was

not used any more in Palestrina's time:  .

Eighth notes were normally used only in groups of two[8] in the sixteenth century. They were introduced and quitted in stepwise movement:

An interval of the fourth, therefore, may be filled out by two eighths
both in ascending and descending motion. The preceding note does
not absolutely need to be a dotted half but may be a quarter:

Auxiliary notes are likewise possible, but only with the lower second.
That the second of two eighths should be a second above the first is
conceivable in the Palestrina style only if the stepwise movement con-

tinues upward, thus:  but not

Furthermore it must be understood that eighths may occur only on
unaccented quarters of the measure. Therefore they cannot come after
a note value greater than a dotted half. Thus procedures such as the
following are foreign to the Palestrina style:

---

8 I have cited a few rare exceptions in *The Style of Palestrina*, pp. 138 f.

Let us turn back to the melody which served as our initial example (p. 84). We note that the repetition of tones occurs scarcely at all. This is, however, rather accidental, for tonal repetition is a very common occurrence in Palestrina melodies, especially with longer note values such as breves, whole notes, and half notes. The matter of tonal repetition depends upon the setting of the text, in that when several different syllables are sung on the same pitch, the note is divided, for example:

With respect to quarter notes, which cannot carry a syllable if they are in succession, there is only one form of repetition in the music of Palestrina: the anticipation approached by step from above. This is very common and, furthermore, may be observed in the seventh and thirteenth measures of the given melody (p. 84). It generally occurs before a syncopated note (as in bar 13), but it does appear quite often without being followed by a suspension. The anticipation usually follows a dotted half, but it may also be found after quarters, for example:

Anticipations may, under all circumstances, come only on unaccented quarters of the measure and (in Palestrina melodies) they are used only when approached by step from above. The anticipation approached from below is often to be found in early Italian composers from the beginning of the sixteenth century and also in the contemporary Netherlanders, as:

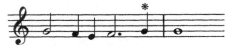

Here, too, the anticipation approached by a descending skip of a third is unusually common, especially with Josquin des Prez, to whom we can almost attribute the most frequent use of this figure, as:

Sta - bat ma - ter do - lo - ro - sa

These early composers also make fairly frequent use of the anticipation approached by a descending skip of a fifth.

In the Palestrina style the attempt to give the melodies harmonic poise, however, never leads to tedious stiffness or to dullness; on the contrary, a certain sprightly energy in the linear treatment is preferred (although completely controlled) and every heaviness and insipid repetition is avoided. Particular care is exercised that the effect of the high tone in the melodic culmination may not be diminished by having that tone occur shortly before, because the culmination itself would thereby be robbed of its force. In the melody discussed we observe accordingly that the culmination note G (bar 11) occurs only this one time and that the other high points do not go beyond the F.[9] Furthermore the culmination point, even when it comes in entirely fresh and achieves its full effect, is not in the least overaccented and does not stand out harshly. We have here one of the best characteristics of the genuine, stylistically pure Palestrina melodies in contrast to later somewhat misguided imitations. Everyone who has even a slight feeling for what is essential and distinctive in this style will be on his guard against a theme such as the following (which is from a motet of J. J. Fux, the so-called "Palestrina of the eighteenth century," who has been mentioned earlier):

Ad te Do - mi - ne le - va - - - - - -

Although everything seems to be in full accord with the laws of the Palestrina style and although this is an excellent and beautiful melody in itself, we can but feel that the total impression has a somewhat modern

---

[9] With respect to the treatment of culmination tones, these may occur at the beginning of melodies, although they rarely do, and at the end, provided the range of the particular melody is not especially large and the movement progresses in such longer note values as whole and half notes. In melodies with quicker rhythms (in halves and quarters) the culmination tone may be repeated, but only if it comes on two tones which are separated by a single tone, as:

sentimental touch which is foreign to a great style. This impression does not depend upon the intervals themselves; the same movements that begin the melody are found (in the same order) in the theme from Palestrina's motet *Surge propera* (see p. 86). It is the rhythm, however, which is the deciding factor here. We shall be much nearer the Palestrina style if we alter the Fux theme somewhat as follows:

The explanation for the less elegant effect that Fux attains may be that in his theme the high tone B-flat in the first curve receives a very strong

accent. It gets this accent because the rhythm ♩. ♩ ♩ , besides underlining the first tone energetically (presumably because this is long in comparison with the following notes), is so arranged that the note is likewise made prominent melodically, that is, as the culmination note B-flat. At the beginning of the third measure the situation becomes still more acute in that, in addition to the rhythmic and melodic accent, there is superimposed a third, namely, a "reminiscent accent" on the high tone D. (That the motive of the second measure is repeated emphasizes it strongly and produces a more pronounced effect because of the higher range.) This last culmination is thereby, so to speak, raised to the third power, and under this threefold accentuation it has an effect like ringing steel—an effect which in its sharpness and exuberance is entirely foreign to the soft and natural linear characteristics of the Palestrina music. It becomes obvious from the foregoing comparison what a decisive rôle rhythm plays in the Palestrina melody [10] and how cautiously and carefully every unusual accentuation of the culmination point is avoided, indeed how everything is shunned which might in any way produce a rough or obtrusive effect. This suggests a comparison with human speech. In this connection I should like to introduce a citation from the textbook on phonetics by the Danish philologist Otto Jespersen: [11]

---

[10] This problem will be treated more in detail in the section on the fifth species (p. 135).
[11] Otto Jespersen: *Lehrbuch der Phonetik,* 2nd Ed. (Leipzig, 1913), p. 229.

. . . The speech of the uncivilized is characterized by great, uncontrolled tonal modulations, while civilization puts a damper on the passions and their expressions in gesture and speech. Politeness demands that one should not use any coarse means in order to call attention to himself; a sensitively educated taste is revealed likewise in a preference for small, fine, expressive nuances in which the outsider is unable to see anything but dull monotony.

Naturally I do not mean that a melody must be as velvety and subdued as possible in order to conform to the ideals of the Palestrina style. On the contrary, it can never be lively and expressive enough. In order to achieve this effect, however, one must, above all, master a certain nuance —I should like to call it the melodic piano. Melodies which continually try to be impressive by the use of excessive movement and the like, are no more able to express genuine emotion than an orchestra can give the impression of real power by constantly playing fortissimo. As in other fields, so here too: he alone will attain really genuine and deep expression who understands the art of restraint.

HARMONY

Although the music of the sixteenth century is based essentially on lines, we must by no means assume that interest in the contrasting dimension, that of chords, was therefore completely lacking.

For the sixteenth century, harmony exists admittedly much more for the sake of linear effects than for its own sake. In order to be able to follow the various melodies in their simultaneous course without difficulty, clearness and beauty in the chordal combinations were required. In the course of the sixteenth century the demand for fullness and independent pleasantness of the harmonies gradually increased. Zarlino already teaches in his work *Istitutioni harmoniche* (1558) that so far as possible the third and fifth (or sixth) should be written over the bass tone. Artusi, indeed, goes so far as to give only complete triads as usable at all in compositions with more than two voices, because, as he expresses it *"la richezza dell' harmonia"* can be attained only in this way. This feeling for "harmonic richness" has doubtless deeply and decisively affected the evolution of music. If one should go through the literature of the Netherland composers of the fifteenth and early sixteenth centuries and on through Palestrina, and then make a tabulation, he would see how the percentage of incomplete and empty combinations constantly decreases and how the filling out of the chords with thirds and sixths simultaneously increases. With Palestrina—apart from more exceptional cases where the melody is built up on the harmony [1] or where the reverse happens—one can always observe a masterful balance in the regard for the melodic and harmonic requirements, although, as I have said, the harmonic demands are generally rather more for the sake of clearness than for anything else.

The same wariness against abrupt or unclear effects which is characteristic of the Palestrina style in the linear treatment is evident in the treatment of chords. Dissonances are used only in restricted forms and in places where they do not produce an obtrusive effect. Their use may be divided into three principal categories:

1. Passing dissonances.

2. Suspension dissonances.

3. Auxiliary dissonances (that is, dissonances which are introduced by step on weak beats and then return to the preceding tone).

In addition to all augmented and diminished intervals, seconds, fourths, sevenths, ninths, and so on, are classed as dissonances. The fourth, however, occupies a very particular, individual position: it hovers between consonance and dissonance and, under certain circumstances which will be discussed later, can be treated as a consonance. But as a rule, the fourth is considered a dissonance. The same thing applies also to other mildly dissonant tonal combinations, such as diminished and augmented fourths and fifths.

In accordance with long-standing tradition, the consonances are divided in the sixteenth century into two groups: perfect and imperfect. The perfect consonances are: unison, fifth, octave, twelfth, and so on; the imperfect consonances are: third, sixth, tenth, and so on. In the sixteenth century, too, perfect consonances are preferred to imperfect at the beginning and end of a composition.

One of the chief theoretical rules of the century forbids the direct progression from one perfect consonance to another. In other words, parallel octaves or fifths are not permissible:

---

[1] Broken chords and the like are very rare in the Palestrina style.

It must be pointed out that this rule applies only where such parallels occur between a given pair of voices; if they are avoided by crossing the voices, then it makes little difference whether or not they are present in the sounds actually heard. A good example is found in the following passage from the Credo of the four-part mass of Palestrina, *In te Domine speravi,* which would sound as follows on the piano:

but which in reality does not have parallel fifths, since it is noted as follows:

Here the fifths are avoided by the crossing of the two upper parts. This is not, as one might assume, purely a matter of form for the sake of evading the rule. On the contrary, it is an expression of the essence of the law, for the tonal quality of the different voices enables one to follow the individual melodies and easily to see that the fifths do not occur in parallel motion.

It is not desirable for two or more fourths to follow each other in similar motion. The only exception is the following progression which, in modern terminology, would be called a series of parallel chords of the sixth:

But progressions such as the following are foreign to the style of Palestrina:

Such procedures are more likely to be found in the Franco-Burgundian composers of the fifteenth century. Thus very common in the work of these masters are cadence formulas such as the following:

The sixteenth century, however, modifies this cadence into the following:

Major thirds, too, are used with a certain cautiousness. Where two voices move in parallel thirds, generally a major third is followed by a minor third because two successive major thirds always produce the tritone effect if the lower part moves a whole tone, as for example:

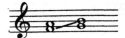

But it would be too strict to forbid the succession of two major thirds entirely. Palestrina himself fairly often uses two and sometimes even three such thirds in direct succession, as in the Gloria of his four-part mass *Lauda Sion,* in which, however, only the last two thirds produce the tritone effect:

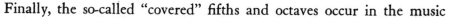

Finally, the so-called "covered" fifths and octaves occur in the music

of Palestrina very rarely in two-part writing, and then they are generally
used in connection with an imitation, as in Palestrina's four-part motet
In diebus illis:

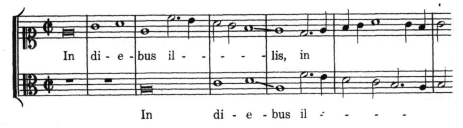

But such fifths and octaves can also occur—even in two-part writing—
without any imitation. In such a case, however, one generally finds that
one of the voices moves by step, as in the following passage from a litany
by Palestrina:

Only rarely in two-part writing do both voices skip in the same direction to a fifth or octave.[2] In general one hesitates to allow two parts to
skip in the same direction unless at least one of the parts is an inner part.

Summary

Although the harmony of the Palestrina style is dominated to a certain
extent by chordal feeling, its full beauty is revealed only in relation
to melodic considerations. Just as we cannot appreciate fully the melody
from Palestrina's offertorium *Ave Maria*, mentioned in the preceding
chapter, so long as it stands alone (for, unlike most modern melodies,
it can very well stand alone), so the harmonic course of the progressions
which we find in this composition, in itself perfectly beautiful and

---

[2] Several characteristic exceptional cases may be found. See my study *"Ueber einen Brief Palestrinas"* mentioned on page 25.

logical, will not produce a profound effect if the relation to the thematic development remains concealed.   Because this work of art was conceived as a whole, it must be perceived as such:

Let us see how everything lives and breathes below this quiet and perhaps slightly classically cool upper voice. Only now does it achieve
color and life.

PART II

Contrapuntal Exercises

INTRODUCTION

MOST OF THE following exercises involve the addition of one or more parts to a given melody, the cantus firmus—a technique which, old as it is, still continues to have decided practical value.

The melodies given below will serve as cantus firmi; but the teacher or the pupil may, if he so chooses, compose for himself similar basic melodies to work with. Note that the melodies given here may be transposed a fourth up or a fifth down (with a signature of one flat) and that they may also be transposed to the upper or lower octave, according to whether they are put in a higher or a lower part. Since, in polyphonic practice, the Lydian mode coincides with the Ionian, only Ionian cantus firmi are indicated. There is of course nothing to prevent those who so desire from experimenting with the Lydian, but they must understand that it does not have any particular practical application. Similarly, the difference between authentic and plagal cantus firmi is disregarded, since it is without significance in polyphonic music.

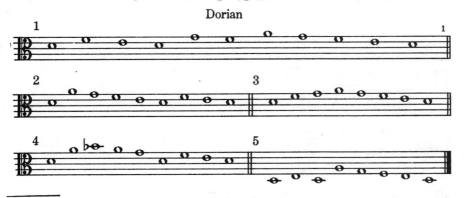

---

[1] The cantus firmi numbers 1, 6, and 20 are by Fux; the others by the author.

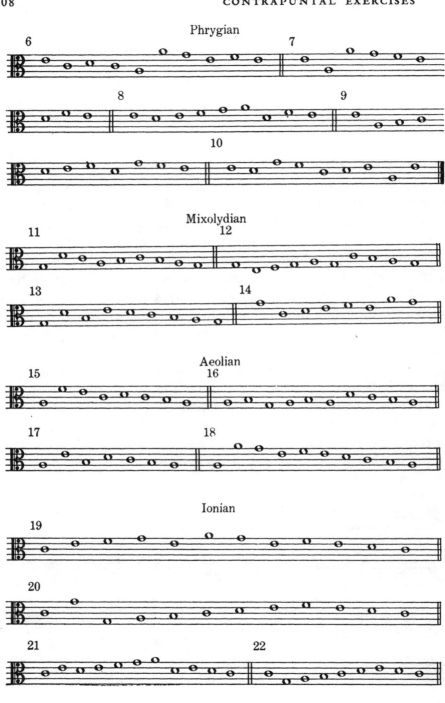

Chapter III

TWO-PART COUNTERPOINT

First Species

IN THE FIRST SPECIES, which is also called "note against note," an upper or lower part is added to the cantus firmus. This added part moves in whole notes as does the cantus firmus. Most important is that this new part (the counterpoint) acquires an independent and beautiful melodic form; under no circumstances may it have the effect of being "contrived" or "forced."

Preliminary Exercise

We shall try to write a single melody in whole notes, confining our-selves to the ecclesiastical modes beginning and ending with either the tonic or the dominant.[1] As already mentioned, all perfect, major, and minor intervals up to the fifths are permitted in ascending as well as in descending motion, as is the perfect octave, whereas the minor sixth is allowed ascending only. The rule that the larger skips must precede the smaller ones in ascending movement while in descending movement the order is reversed must not be applied too rigidly where the movement takes place in whole notes (each whole note receiving two counts); but it is well to observe it whenever possible. The melody must be quiet and sure in its movement, so that it is felt as an individuality which knows where it is going and not as a mere victim of circumstances wan-dering willy-nilly here and there. A melody like the following has a vague and cramped effect; it lacks "direction":

---

[1] It should be emphasized again that, in the "polyphonic" ecclesiastical modes, the fifth above the tonic is always the dominant (see page 71).

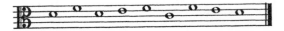

In the main, the dull impression must be considered as due to the circumstance that the melody seems to stick at the highest note F without
being able to go beyond it. If the sixth note C is replaced by a G, the
result is very much better. The melody does not become really good, for
there are still too many F's in it, but it does acquire, nevertheless, something of a musical character. Naturally a melody which possesses
"direction" is not necessarily beautiful—a guaranteed procedure for the
production of beautiful melodies does not exist (fortunately!). That the
following melody, although well defined in contour, has an inartistic and
monotonous effect may be admitted without argument:

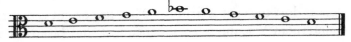

A stepwise progression is good enough in itself, but scales alone are
not sufficient. It is a question of creating melodies clear in design and
at the same time varied in the assortment of tones used. It is especially
important, as has already been mentioned, that the highest tone be used
in a fresh and effective way; therefore it is well to avoid introducing this
tone more than once—especially where the melodies are fairly short, as
in these exercises. One should exercise similar caution in the treatment
of the lowest tone. Although it is not so important as the highest tone,
it demands a certain amount of consideration; hence it is best not to
repeat this note too frequently in the melody—in any case not without
a considerable interval of time intervening. It is moreover necessary
to keep each separate part within a reasonable or singable range. We
assume the exercises for chorus, and therefore we do not let the soprano

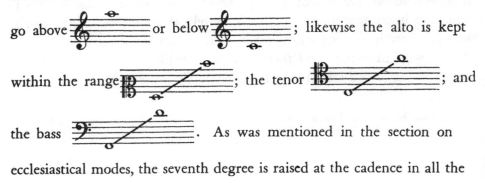

ecclesiastical modes, the seventh degree is raised at the cadence in all the scales except the Phrygian, in which half steps do not already exist between the seventh and eighth degrees. In a cadence it is not so good to approach the seventh degree (leading tone) by an ascending skip as to introduce it by a stepwise progression, but it is permissible to approach

it by a descending skip of a third. Therefore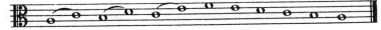

is not permissible, but is acceptable. Much better is this:

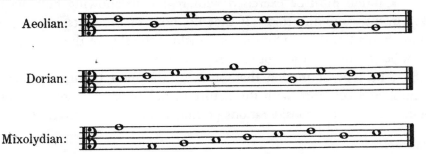

In melodic construction, too many skips are bad; a melody which is constantly skipping is no melody at all. Likewise we must be careful of sequences, since they generally sound very trivial. Fux's Aeolian cantus firmus, for example, is less useful on this account.[2]

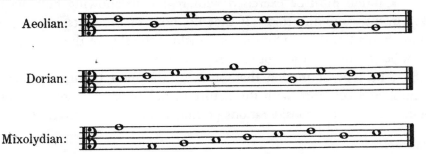

On the other hand, melodies like the following are good:

Aeolian:

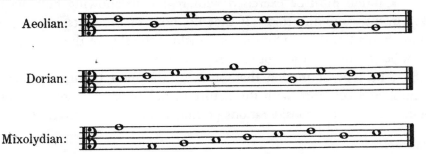

Dorian:

Mixolydian:

The repetition of a tone is permitted occasionally in the first species, and there only.

Counterpoint

Bearing in mind so far as possible the melodic considerations just discussed, let us add parts above and below the given cantus firmus, proceeding according to the following rules:

1. Only consonant combinations may be used. (Do not forget that the fourth is considered a dissonance.)

---

[2] To this must be added that the beginning suggests broken chords (compare p. 98).

2. One must begin and end with a perfect consonance (octave, fifth, and so on). If the counterpoint lies in the lower part, however, only the octave or unison may be used at the beginning and ending.

3. Unisons may occur only on the first and last notes of the cantus firmus.

4. Hidden and parallel fifths and octaves are not permitted. It is therefore not permissible to approach a fifth or octave in similar motion.

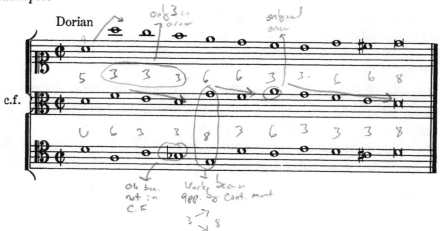

5. The cantus firmus and counterpoint must not be too far apart. Only for the sake of a beautiful voice leading should the interval of the tenth be exceeded.

6. The counterpoint and cantus firmus must not move in parallel thirds and sixths for too long at a time, since the independence of the counterpoint is thereby destroyed. It is, to be sure, hard to fix a definite limit; but more than four such parallels are not good where the voices, as in this species, move in whole notes.

7. Caution must be exercised with regard to allowing both parts to skip in the same direction. If they do, none of the parts ought to skip more than a fourth. (This does not include the skip of the octave, which must be considered a sort of tone repetition.)

8. The type of motion that produces the most beautiful effect and is most in accordance with the nature of polyphony is contrary motion. Wherever melodic considerations permit, it should be preferred.

Examples

Phrygian

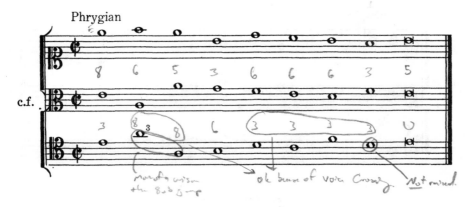

Mixolydian

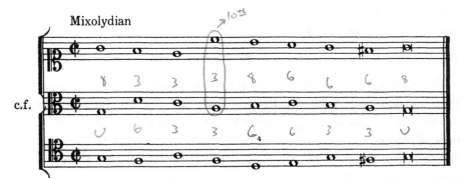

Aeolian

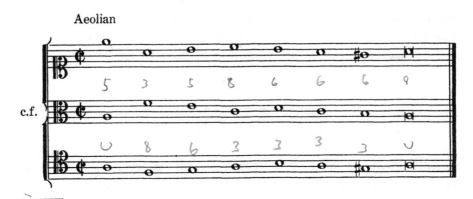

---

[3] To "cross" the parts (occasionally to let the lower part go above the upper part or vice versa) is a technique which cannot be recommended sufficiently. One may say that without this no real polyphony is possible.

[4] Two skips of a third in the same direction are permissible and are not regarded as an arpeggio.

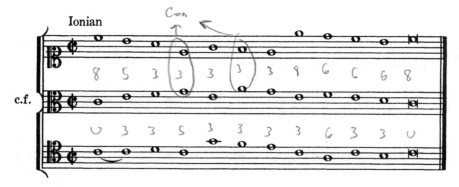

SECOND SPECIES

In these exercises two notes are set in the counterpoint against each note in the cantus firmus.

Preliminary Exercise

Write melodies in half notes. It is permissible to begin with an up-beat; in such cases, however, the first tone must be the tonic or the fifth of the scale. Likewise in the next to the last and third to the last measures, a whole note may be substituted for the two half notes, while the last note in this as in all other species must invariably be a breve. The repetition of a tone, being permissible only in the first species (see p. 111), is accordingly forbidden in the second and in the remaining species. The rule previously mentioned about the succession of larger and smaller intervals in the same direction must be observed more carefully here than where (as in the first species) the movement takes place in whole notes; however an idiom like the following may be used:

but only when the descending progression of the second follows immediately after the ascending skip of the third, which is introduced contrary to rule. The following procedure is not so good:

However, it may be used.   But in the style under consideration, a melodic line such as the following is lacking in form and design:

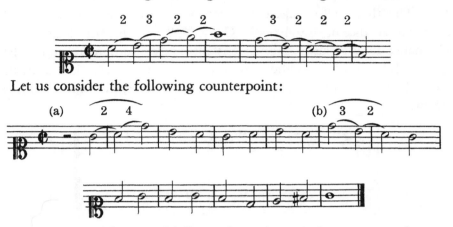

Let us consider the following counterpoint:

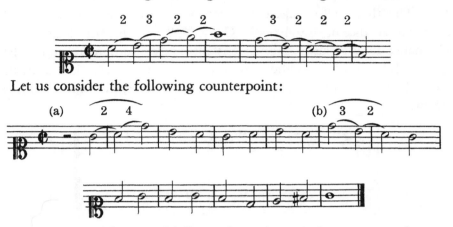

It seems unsatisfactory chiefly, perhaps, because it appears to be constantly knocking its head against the twice-lined D without ever achieving a climax that seems natural and free.   To this must be added also the irregular progressions of intervals at (a) and (b) in combination with a monotonous use of the tonal material (among the twenty-two notes of the melody in question, the notes which lie closely adjoining—B, A, G, F [F-sharp]—occur, respectively, 3, 5, 6, and 4 times).   Furthermore the repetition of the tonal material in the eighth and ninth measures is monotonous.   Such redundancy (as well as sequences) must be definitely avoided.   It is especially important in these short melodies to strive for good classical style, which implies the strictest economy of melodic material and the avoidance of all padding.   With the following changes the preceding melody becomes acceptable:

Counterpoint

In trying to combine such a melody in half notes with a cantus firmus, we must observe the following rules:

1. The arsis (the accented portion of the measure) may have only consonance.

2. The thesis (the unaccented portion of the measure) may have either consonance or dissonance.[5]   Consonance may be introduced freely; dissonance may be used only if it is introduced conjunctly and is left conjunctly continuing in the same direction (in this way it fills in the interval of the third between the two notes on either side of it), as follows:

but not:

Here, to be sure, a dissonance is introduced conjunctly and proceeds conjunctly, but in the opposite direction from that in which it was introduced.   The following methods of treatment are of course entirely inadmissible:

3. The unison on the strong accent is permissible only on the first and the last notes of the cantus firmus.   In the remainder of the counter-

---

[5] It is to be noted here once and for all that all the rules in this manual are based on the premise that the half note is the unit of measure (it takes one beat).

point, however, it may also be used on the unaccented portion of the
measure. It should be noted in this connection that it is best that the
unison introduced by skip be quitted by conjunct motion in the opposite
direction, although this may not always be possible.

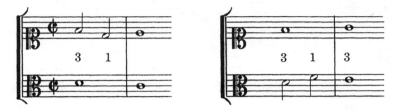

4. Accented fifths or octaves (fifths or octaves following each other
on successive accents) must be used carefully, even if they are not
excluded entirely.

Examples

Dorian

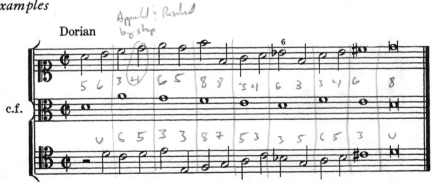

c.f.

---

[6] Since bar lines are superfluous in exercises with cantus firmi, we shall not use them in this
book. One should observe that when bar lines are not used, accidentals apply only to the note
immediately following.

Phrygian

Mixolydian

Aeolian

Ionian

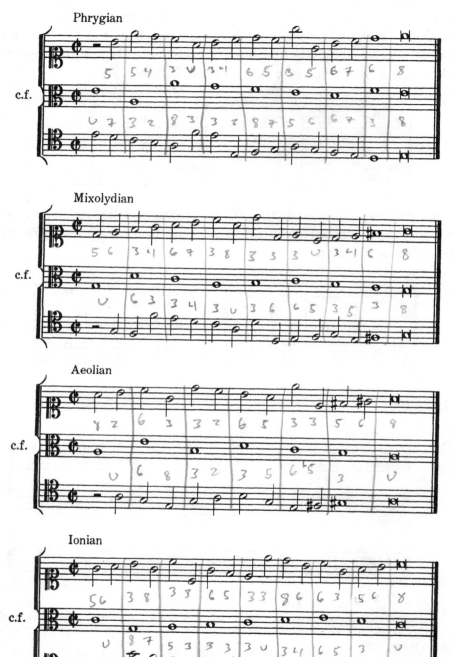

Triple time with the half note as the unit of measure requires, in the Palestrina style, that each half note be a consonance. It is, therefore, not in accordance with the laws of the style when Bellermann, Haller, and others permit the second and third half to be dissonant. The rule is that in triple time only the second half of each unit of measure may be dissonant. Thus in 3/1 time only every other half note may be dissonant and in 3/2 time every other quarter. Consequently, only by the notation are 3/1 time and 3/2 time distinguished, and there is therefore no reason for treating triple time before the following exercises in third species.

THIRD SPECIES

In these exercises four quarters are to be set against each note in the cantus firmus.

Preparatory Exercise

First, write exercises in quarter-note movement. As in the preceding species, it is permissible to begin with an up-beat, therefore with a quarter rest, and occasionally also with a rest of two or three quarters. In the next to the last bar, two half notes or one whole note may be substituted for the four quarters, while the last measure, as in all species, must have a breve. With note values as comparatively short as quarter notes, it is necessary, as I have said, to observe all the melodic rules more rigidly than with slower rhythms, because one is more conscious of the melodic context in the more rapidly moving notes. In these exercises, therefore, no exceptions are permitted to the rule that larger intervals must precede smaller ones in continuous ascending movement, and vice versa, where the direction is opposite. Nor are two or more successive skips in the same direction permitted.[7] But even where the correct succession of larger and smaller movements in the same direction is observed, the possibilities with quarter notes are much more limited than with the greater note values. In reality only two usable combinations are available: the ascending third followed by its upper second, for example:

---

[7] Compare p. 89.

and the descending step of the second followed by the skip of the third
in the same direction, for example:

If, in this case, a fourth is substituted for the skip of the third,
the limits for this style have already been violated. A figure like

 is therefore most rare in Palestrina, and with the

downward skip of the fourth, for example ⟨music⟩ , it
does not occur at all.

Furthermore, the rule that no upward skips from an accented quarter
note are permissible must be closely observed. Therefore, movements
like the following must be avoided:

On the other hand the inversions of these figures are quite permissible:

Likewise, one must take care as far as possible to fill out skips im-

mediately. A figure such as ⟨music⟩ is best continued thus:

⟨music⟩ , but may also be continued by upward skips, for
example:

but under no circumstances by continuous downward movement.

Likewise of great significance is the rule which is partially covered by
what has already been said (compare p. 92) and according to which
an unaccented quarter note, introduced stepwise from below, is preferably
continued upward by step, hence treated as a passing note. Violations

of this rule are very rare; the only fairly usual exception to this rule is the descending skip of the third following an unaccented quarter note introduced stepwise from below, for example:

The unaccented quarter note introduced *from above* is treated with greater freedom. The best proof for this is the much-liked *cambiata* figure:  But also comparatively common figures like the following:

serve to illustrate the same point.

Sequences like  must of course be avoided.

Generally, descending skips from two successive accented quarter notes are not so good (if they are ascending, they are of course still worse). Repetition of the tone of the first quarter on the third quarter has a trivial effect if the third quarter is introduced from above. The same holds true under similar circumstances for repetitions of the second to the fourth quarter. Therefore, idioms like the following are rarely or never met with in the stylistically pure music of Palestrina:

while such repetitions of tone may pass where the third or the fourth quarter note is introduced from below. For example, the following ornament is exceedingly popular and common in the sixteenth century:

---

[8] It is to be noted, however, that a skip of the third downward from an unaccented quarter note, irrespective of the other rhythmic circumstances, must always be followed by a step of the second upward.

Likewise idioms such as:

are in constant favor in the sixteenth century, even if the height of their popularity lies somewhat further back.

In this species unusual possibilities for beautiful melodic progressions are afforded, and it is now important to use them so that the structure of the melodies in the broader sense of the word may become beautiful and artistic. It is impossible to give a definite outline for the architecture of such a melody—even within a style so definitely circumscribed as that of the time of Palestrina melodies may be written in a thousand different ways and yet each be good. A particularly beautiful form, however, is the one that has its climax (highest note) toward the end of the melody and gradually reaches its culmination in a soft and natural chain of smaller ascents and descents:

It is inadvisable to put the point of culmination at the very end of the melody; it may easily have the effect of a sudden and dramatic conclusion. It would be better to place the culmination note at the beginning of the melody, although even then it might be difficult to bring about the necessary tranquillity and balance.

Not to criticize, which in most cases is a relatively easy matter when a system of teaching has reached a certain age, but to demonstrate the contrast between the older counterpoint, more harmonically based and the newer of stronger melodic tendencies, we will take from Fux an example which later has gone into more modern manuals:

Lydian

Although one cannot deny that this melody manifests a certain sureness in the linear treatment (it reaches its climax, a¹, for example, by means of a logical and purposeful ascent), nevertheless, it is strongly marked by purely harmonic impulses. Thus we find in the second measure, a G major chord of the sixth sketched in (which, moreover, is contrary to the rule constantly observed in the style of Palestrina that in quarter-note movement two skips in the same direction are not to be written). In the same way measures 5 to 7 are to be regarded as figurations of the harmonic

progressions   because of the sequential way in

which the skip of the third is accented (measure 7 has the same motive as 5 to 6, but in reverse order). Measure 9 has a still more awkward effect because it not only consists of a sequence (the repeated skip of the third: C–E) but also twice violates the rule that there should be no upward skip from an accented quarter note. This last rule, which was not quite clear to the earlier students of the style, is violated, moreover, in measures 2 and 7, as well as 4. It is generally evident how harmonic considerations have carried too much weight here. Only by "thinking horizontally" is it possible to reach a genuine polyphonic manner of writing.

Counterpoint

The rules for the chordal combinations in this species are as follows:

1. On the first and the third quarters of the measure, only consonances may be used. Concerning this rule, Fux remarks that occasionally (only, however, when the first, second, and fourth quarters are consonant) the third quarter may be dissonant. However, this rule, adopted by most

of the manuals founded on Fux, is not borne out in the style of Palestrina.[9]
A few exceptions which, in two-part counterpoint, can occur only when
both voices move freely (but not when, as in this case, one voice is restricted to whole-note movement) will be mentioned later on.

2.   On the second and fourth quarter, dissonance may be used.   The
conditions under which this may occur are, as in the second species, the
stepwise introduction and continuation of the dissonance.   But while it
was possible in half-note movement to use only the so-called "passing note
dissonances," in the third species one is not restricted to the continuation
in the *same* direction, but may return to the tone from which one started;
in other words, it is permissible here to use dissonant auxiliary notes.
Fux, to be sure, does not use such dissonances, and Bellermann says in this
regard: [10]

> The composers of the sixteenth century likewise knew this kind of dissonance
> but they rarely used it, and then only in notes of shorter value, quarters and eights.

With this remark Bellermann forbids their use henceforth.   Meanwhile
he is definitely in error when he asserts that this procedure is rare in the
sixteenth century.   On the contrary, it is very popular.   From a thousand
or more examples, let us take the following from the beginning of
Palestrina's four-part motet *Magnum haereditatis mysterium:*

The third quarter in the fourth measure in the excerpt above does not
continue the conjunct descending movement started on the first and
second quarters, as it should have done according to the rules concerning
the treatment of dissonance as formerly given, but returns to the starting
note A by which the dissonance G on the second quarter takes a turn, as
it were, around the A, becoming thereby a returning (auxiliary) note.

---

[9] Credit for having proved this convincingly goes to the German theorist Franz Nekes, who,
in a review of Haller's *Kompositionslehre* in *"Gregorius Blatt"* 1892, points out this relation clearly.
[10] *Kontrapunkt,* p. 154.

Note, however, that while this type of dissonance is very common in the style of Palestrina when the auxiliary dissonance is the second below the preceding accented quarter note, the contrary is the case where the auxiliary note is the second above. It follows, moreover, from what has

been said earlier under "Melody," that idioms like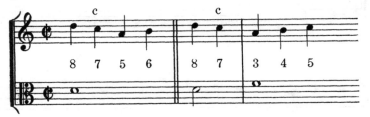

were already avoided for purely melodic considerations.[11] There was all the more reason to avoid this type of idiom when, in addition, there was a possibility of threatening the harmonic beauty of the composition with a relatively strongly marked dissonance. In the present exercises we will, therefore, allow the lower auxiliary dissonance. The upper auxiliary dissonance cannot be used when, as in this case, the movement takes place exclusively in quarter notes. Counterpoint in mixed note values presents to a certain extent a different problem—of which more will be said later.

The main rule for the treatment of dissonance in quarter-note movement is, therefore, that they must fall on the unaccented part of the measure and must be introduced and continued stepwise. There is, however, one and only one fairly common exception to the rule about the stepwise continuation of the dissonances: the so-called *cambiata*. By this term is meant the idiom in which the dissonance introduced stepwise from above (which, like all dissonance in this and the preceding species, falls on the unaccented part of the measure) is quitted by the skip of the third downward followed by the step of the second upward, for example:

3. It is also the rule in the third species, as in the preceding species, to begin with the perfect consonance. If, however, the counterpoint begins with the up-beat, imperfect consonances may be used occasionally

4. Aside from the first and last measures, the unison is not allowed on

---

[11] Compare p. 91.

the first quarter of the measure but may be used freely on the remaining beats.

5.   Accented fifths or octaves on successive accented quarters following each other may be permitted very rarely.   Especially octaves such as the following are so flat as to be practically unusable.

If they are four quarters apart, they are acceptable, especially in the following cadence:

The same applies to the fifths.

Examples

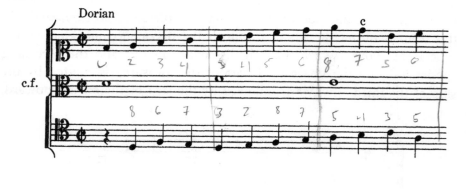

Phrygian

c.f.

Mixolydian

c.f.

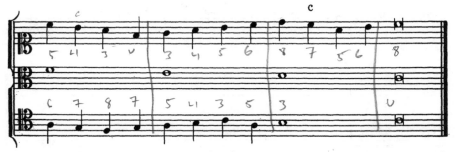

The rules for binary meters apply also to ternary meters. For example:

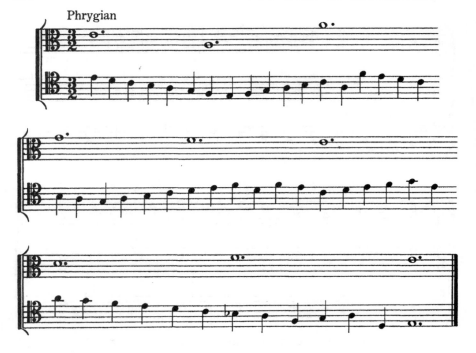

FOURTH SPECIES

In the fourth species, as in the second, two half notes are written in the counterpoint against each note in the cantus firmus. In contrast to the practice in the second species, the unaccented half note is tied to the accented one immediately following, so that a chain of suspensions is formed. Thus in reality the counterpoint moves in whole notes in the same way as in the first species, and the same melodic rules apply here as there. The rules for the sequence of larger and smaller intervals in the same direction may be interpreted much more freely in the fourth species than in the first. The melodic continuity is weakened by the formation of the syncopations, and the exercises of the fourth species have, therefore, more vertical character in contrast to those of the preceding species, because they serve mainly as practice in the use of suspension dissonances, while they emphasize linear aspects to a much lesser extent. Consequently we may disregard here specific melodic preparatory exercises.

The more important rules for the chordal combinations are as follows:

1. Dissonances may be used only on accented half notes, and so used that the dissonant tone is tied over from the unaccented part of the preceding measure, where it must be a consonance with the cantus firmus. After that it must be taken stepwise downward to a consonance on the unaccented part of the measure, for example:

While the dissonances in the preceding species are placed only on unaccented parts of the measure where they are less noticed and pass by more easily, the fourth species follows exactly the opposite procedure: it uses the dissonance for its own sake. Here we want expressly to hear dissonance and dissonance only; presumably in order to be able to enjoy the artistically valuable contrast between consonance and dissonance. In the second and third species, the dissonances were only tolerated. Nevertheless, even if in the fourth species we wish to have the dissonance placed so that it stands out clearly, we must be constantly on the alert for acrid or obtrusive effects. Consequently the dissonance must be "prepared"; that is, the dissonant tone must be tied over from the unaccented part of the preceding measure where it is introduced as consonance. Because the dissonant tone is thus felt in consonant relation to the cantus firmus immediately before the harsh effect takes place, any shock is removed, and also the stepwise descending resolution—perhaps one of the most quieting musical effects—serves to tone down and smooth out the roughness.

2. Dissonances may be resolved only to imperfect consonances. One wants to hear after dissonance a really full and harmonious effect; therefore one resolves to a third, sixth, tenth, and the like, but not so well to "empty" fifths and octaves. It follows, therefore, in connection with the demand for stepwise descending resolution, that with the counterpoint in the upper voice, only the seventh and fourth may be used as a suspension dissonance; and with counterpoint below the cantus firmus only the second and ninth, as follows:

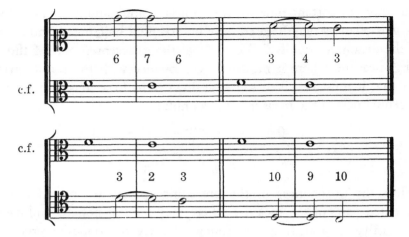

Accordingly, in two-part counterpoint, the ninth and second in the upper voice and fourth and seventh in the lower part should be disregarded entirely, since they all resolve into perfect consonances: [12]

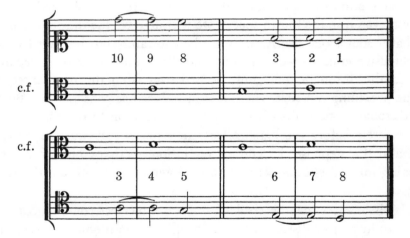

3. In the fourth species as many suspension dissonances as possible are used. However, out of regard for the voice leading and for the harmonic progressions, it is occasionally necessary to put a consonance on the arsis. In this case the continuation of the syncopating tone is optional, for example:

---

[12] Similarly one ought to avoid all augmented and diminished intervals in suspensions.

c.f.

The stepwise descending continuation is obligatory only where the syncope is dissonant.

4.   If a syncopated consonance occurs on the strong accent it is permissible to take a passing dissonance on the following weak beat, but only in accordance with the rules of second species,[13] for example:

Occasionally it may be necessary to break the chain of syncopations. To do so gives rise to episodes of the second species which are handled according to the rules of this species, for example:

c.f.

5.   The unison may be used freely in the fourth species both on arsis and thesis.   If the suspensions are broken, the rules of the second species hold also with respect to unisons.

6.   It is permissible to begin with the up-beat, which then must form a perfect consonance to the cantus firmus.

7.   In the fourth species, if the counterpoint lies in the upper voice, it is best to use the suspension of the seventh in the cadence; with the cantus firmus in the upper voice, the suspension of the second is the rule.

_____

[13] See pp. 116 f.

Where it is demanded by the cantus firmus, however, one may put a whole note in the next to the last measure.

Examples

Dorian

c.f.

Phrygian

c.f.

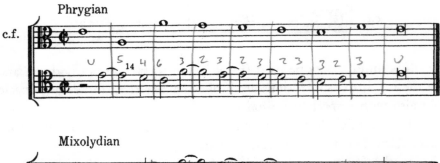

Mixolydian

c.f.

---

14 Compare p. 142.

FIFTH SPECIES

Preparatory Exercise

Write melodies with mixed note values.

In the fifth and most important species of all, for which the preceding exercises are only preparatory, the rhythm is free; that is, we are no longer limited to one specific note value, but may use breves, whole notes, half notes, quarters, or eighths. These note values, however, may not be used *ad libitum;* the rhythms also as well as the intervals are subject to certain artistic laws. When melody and rhythm unite the relation becomes very complex and subtle. It becomes increasingly difficult to formulate impressions into rules; they must be held fluid within certain broad limits. We will therefore limit ourselves to a few generalizations. In spite of all efforts, an "aesthetic of rhythm" is still well in the future.

1. It is important to create variety in the melodies; consequently the note values must be arranged so that the impression is at once both fresh and flexible. Everything which might have a stiff and abrupt effect must be avoided. Only a poor melody would have the first four measures in half notes, the next four in quarter notes, and so forth. Such a melody would seem awkward and lacking in continuity. It would be still worse to fill the first four measures with whole notes and the next four with quarter notes, since rhythmic contrasts should not be so juxtaposed but should be introduced smoothly and evenly. Just as the intervals demand a balanced treatment so that after larger skips smaller movements are introduced and vice versa, so rhythms require compensation: after longer note values a need is felt for shorter ones. A classical example of such

a completely beautiful rhythmic balance is the famous beginning of the
Sanctus in Palestrina's *Marcellus Mass:*

San - - - - - - - ctus, San - - - - -

After the smoothly introduced syncope in measures 1 to 2, the receding
movement of the two quarters in the second measure is felt as a natural
resolution, which, however, contains the elastic power for continuation.
With increasing rhythmic and melodic energy the movement continues
in measure three, and leads by virtue of its organic development to the
extremely expressive and nobly accentuated climax on G. The melody
consists of three curves one above (or around) the other, and the way
in which the more rapid movements are here developed from the slower
ones, the higher curves from the lower, has almost the quality of a natural
phenomenon, in the sense that in its presence one feels a deep conviction
that inevitably it must be just so, as when a stone falling into a pool produces rings in wider and wider circles. Most of all, perhaps, the tranquil
and natural use of this theme reminds one of a noble and gracefully
splashing fountain.

The syncope which plays such a decisive rôle in the melody above is
constantly felt as a rhythmic element which requires some special compensation because of the halting effect which it produces in the movement.
Often, therefore, shorter note values are put immediately before the syncope as in the following example, with its anticipation figure:

Similarly, it is a favorite practice to allow the syncopated note to be
followed by eighths:

2. It is important to create "organic" melodies of unbreakable continuity. Therefore, to develop the faster movements gradually from the
slower ones and (especially in the cadence) the slower from the faster

is good. As has been pointed out, the excerpt from the *Marcellus Mass*
ingeniously shows such a transition from quieter to more lively movements, but almost every beginning theme in compositions of the sixteenth
century is of this type.   An especially beautiful example of such a rhythmic crescendo with a consequent decrescendo is found at the beginning
of Palestrina's four-part motet *Valde honorandus est:*

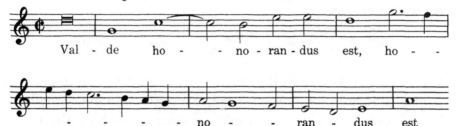

At first glance, one might think that the composer proceeded in a
pedantic and mechanical way, since he puts a breve in the first measure,
whole notes in the second, and half notes very methodically in the third.
However, no dry calculation lies behind this procedure; everything is
inspiration.   Try once to sing this melody and feel how well it fits the
words, how beautifully and naturally it expresses them!   Likewise it is
worth while to note how the climax is formed rhythmically and melodically in the same way as in the melody given above from the *Marcellus
Mass.*   There is, moreover, something very natural in this tendency to
dwell on the higher notes, especially when they are accentuated.   As an
experiment let us undertake to rhythmize the following descending series:

How much more beautiful the effect is when one lingers on its highest
note than when one begins with the more rapid note values and thereafter goes over to the slower ones, for example:

In the last case the whole is felt to be a bit awkward and short of
breath, while the form in *Valde honorandus est* has a free and natural

effect. What also serves to make the latter form so beautiful is that, descending from measure 4 to 5, it rests on two rhythmically varied portions of the measure, since the first note falls on the third (accented) half note of the measure, while the fifth note falls on the second (unaccented) half note of the measure. The effect would be much less pronounced if both rests were laid on rhythmically similar parts of the measure, for example:

The striking difference in the treatment of ascending and descending movement which we have observed earlier meets us also in the rhythmic field. Though it is best in descending movement to have the longer note values come before the shorter ones, it is quite correct in ascending movement to begin with the quicker notes. The following is fairly common:

especially where, as here, the last note in the ascending series is suspended; but at least just as frequently one finds:

while the inversion of this figure:

is seldom seen, since the corresponding melodic situation is almost always balanced as follows:

---

15 It is almost as though one had submitted himself involuntarily to the law of gravity and other natural laws. If we liken the lowest tone to the surface of the earth, then the same phenomenon occurs that we observe when a falling body moves with constantly increasing speed as it approaches the earth; and the fact that one moves faster at the beginning of an ascent than when he has gone part of the way seems to be illustrated here.

The following applies further to the treatment of quarters:

3. *a.* It is best generally if the quarter-note movement begins on the unaccented half note. This rule applies especially to descending movements; where melodies ascend and consequently the lesser note values may well precede the greater, a quarter-note movement may begin on the accent. If one descends thus in quarter notes from such an accented half note, the most natural form is the stepwise, for example:

One can, however, advantageously use also figures such as:

If, on the contrary, melodies ascend in a similar manner, the direct scalewise procedure has a somewhat sharp effect:

and is only infrequently found in works from the florescent period of vocal polyphony.[16] It is much better here to place a skip downward at the beginning. Then, by the law of balance, it moves naturally in the opposite direction. Especially fine is the following idiom:

but also with fourth, fifth, and even octave skips the figure is excellent, for example:

b. It is best, as a rule, if the quarter-note movement continues up to an accented half note, hence rather:

---

[16] This is quite in keeping with the idea that a certain thrusting energy is required in order to get the ascending movement, which offers the greatest resistance, under way again after the halt on the accented part of the measure (where it is especially noticeable).

Even with the best composers of the sixteenth century, one finds, however, idioms of the last-mentioned type, but most often in such cases, the
unaccented half note holds over to form a suspension before which the
quarter-note movement stops, thus:

c. Even if one will tolerate more quarters in succession than half or
whole notes, naturally a time comes when one desires other rhythms.
It is difficult here to set any definite limit; but a selection like the following (taken from the Credo of Palestrina's *Missa sine titulo,* Vol. 24,
in his complete works) may approximately suggest the maximum number
of successive quarter notes:

d. Preferably two quarters should not stand isolated in the place of an
accented half note in a bar. In order to make such a movement less
asthmatic in effect, it is necessary to add quarter notes either before or
after. Therefore not:

but:

However, the two "accented" quarters can remain, too, if the subsequent
half note is suspended:

<hr />

17 See p. 88.

or if the first of the two quarters is tied over to the preceding half note:

4. Concerning the treatment of eighth notes, there is nothing to be added here to what was said in the section on melody (pp. 93 f.).

5. In regard to syncopation:

a. The note of least value to be syncopated with another note of equal value is the half note. Therefore a quarter note cannot be tied to a quarter, for example:

b. It is not permissible to tie notes of less value to subsequent notes of greater value:  . The opposite may take place,

but in such a case only values can be tied that are in relation to each other at 2:1. In other words, one can dot breves, whole notes, half notes, or quarter notes, but one cannot use the double dot, which one would be obliged to do if (according to sixteenth century practice) one wished to write the following rhythms without the bar line:

The rule that shorter values may not be tied to longer has no validity when it is the last note to which the former is tied.

In the use of dotted half notes the rules for the third species apply to the last third of the note value. Therefore the following quarter note

---

18 As a precaution I should like to call attention to the footnote on page 116. The rule stated above applies only where the half note is the unit of measure. In four-four time, which is often used in the madrigal music of the sixteenth century, there is nothing to prevent the suspension of one quarter to the next.

may be either a passing dissonance or a dissonant auxiliary note, for example:

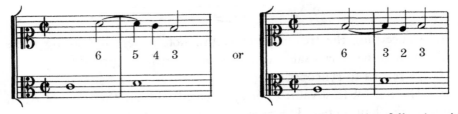

It may not, however, proceed upward by skip. Hence, the following is not permissible:

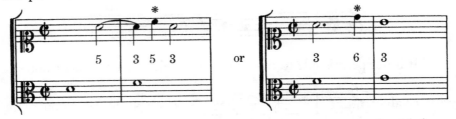

A theme of Palestrina will indicate what we are concerned with better than all these rules. From a great many possibilities I choose one of the most beautiful, a fragment of the four-part motet *Ego sum panis vivus:*

Let it speak for itself. Whoever fully understands the lucid and unexcelled masterpiece that this apparently simple melody represents has in reality learned more than all theorists and rules of style can teach.

Counterpoint

The rules for the preceding four species also apply to the fifth as far as the dissonance treatment is concerned. As a result of the additional possibilities afforded in this species by the use of dotted notes, some cases arise that are not covered by the preceding rules. Thus, the unaccented half note that follows after a tie or after a whole note can form a dissonance when the dissonance is treated according to the rules of the second species (but half notes of this kind may not be dissonant, if preceded by a quarter).

The same applies to quarter notes after ties or dotted half notes.

It is further necessary to observe that quarter notes which are tied over from preceding unaccented half notes should rarely be used as dissonances.[19] Wrong:

Right:

On the other hand, a suspended quarter note can dissonate on a weak beat of the measure in either descending or ascending stepwise movement:[20]

In general it is better, however, for both voices to proceed conjunctly as in the foregoing example. While in the fifth species (as well as in the third species where the movement is entirely in quarter notes[21]) it is not permissible to let the third quarter in the measure dissonate, it is another matter when the note that is dissonating follows after an accented half note (not after a quarter note) and the melodic movement all the way through is stepwise downward. While this:

is absolutely forbidden, the following is unobjectionable.

---

[19] Translator's note. Except, of course, in the ornamental resolution of the dissonance suspension. See p. 148.

[20] I mention this here although it can first occur in free two-part writing.

[21] Compare p. 123.

5   4   3

In other words, when two quarters move in stepwise progression down-ward, if the movement follows an accented half note, it is permissible to let the first (or second) of these quarters dissonate. If, on the other hand, the motion is stepwise ascending, for example:

6   7   8

(which, as we already know, is not so good on purely melodic grounds) then only the second of these quarters may dissonate. In contrast to the third species, in which the lower auxiliary dissonance only was per-mitted,[22] in the fifth species the upper auxiliary dissonance also may be used, though only when it precedes a half or a whole note. For example:[23]

6   7   6   7

We have until now had to do with the *cambiata* in the quarter-note movement only, according to the rules of third species.[24] It also appears in some rhythmic forms which occur more frequently in free composition than the one already mentioned:

or

In all such cases, however, the dissonant note itself (the second note of the *cambiata*) can have only the value of a quarter note. If the third note of the *cambiata* is a quarter, the fourth note also must have that value, and in such cases the fifth note must necessarily be the upper second to

22 Compare p. 125.
23 See *The Style of Palestrina and the Dissonance*, p. 162.
24 See p. 125.

the fourth. If the third note of the *cambiata* is a half note (it can in general be only a half note or a quarter), the next note can be a half or a whole note. In such cases, the fourth note of the *cambiata* need not be led on stepwise upward, but may be treated freely as in the following excerpt from Palestrina's four-part motet *Misit Herodes:*

The genetic history of the *cambiata* may be briefly outlined as follows: This figure goes back originally to a sort of decorative note with which the downward skip of the fourth was adorned, where in place of

 was put . In this case one

was not so particular if the second note (in the expanded form) was dissonant here and there and did not demand subsequent resolution of the dissonance.

Thus at the end of the fifteenth and the beginning of the sixteenth century, a very popular cadence was as follows:

Jacob Obrecht (ca. 1430-1505). Mass: Je ne demande.

Originally the *cambiata* figure consisted of only three notes. If, as in the example above, one did not conclude with the third note, one could put as the fourth note any one of the following: the second, third, or fourth below, or the third, fourth, fifth, minor sixth, or octave above the third note. In the fifteenth century, however, a form that could be called the "classical" was known. This form was the one with the step of the second upward after the third note, for example:

Dufay (ca. 1400-1474).   Mass : Se la face ay pale.

Well into the sixteenth century this form supplants all the others, and in the style of Palestrina, it is actually used exclusively. Undoubtedly the reason for this is that in this style the law or rule about the stepwise continuation of dissonances is applied practically without exception. While the other *cambiata* forms obviously contradict this rule, the "classical" form is only an apparent exception to it, and may therefore stand even under the more strict interpretation of the laws of the style. Since the third tone of the *cambiata* goes to its upper second, the latter is felt to be the note of resolution even if it occurs late, and the third note is thought of as a nonessential ornamental insertion, which is not able to hide the real and perfectly normal treatment of the dissonance, namely, its stepwise continuation.

At the same time that the freer *cambiata* forms mentioned above are supplanted, the "ascending" *cambiata* disappears. This figure, which is the exact inversion of the classical *cambiata* (and in which, therefore, the dissonance is introduced stepwise from *below* and is continued by the skip of the third *upward,* followed by a step of the second *downward*) was common around the year 1500. For example:

Josquin des Prez (ca. 1450-1521). Mass: Hercules.

The only slightly irregular form of the *cambiata* which is fairly common in Palestrina, especially in his earlier works, is the idiom which might be called the "extended" *cambiata,* for example:

Palestrina, Motet: Magnum haereditatis mysterium.

As may be seen from the example given above, the third note of the *cambiata* is followed by the skip of the third upward, followed in turn by a step of the second downward, through which the real note of resolution comes at last and is thus doubly delayed.[25] In this way the

[25] The English theorist Kitson puts things upside down when he says about the "free" and "extended" *cambiate,* as they are found in the composers of the sixteenth century: ". . . through constant use, the real significance of the Nota Cambiata has been forgotten." Kitson, C. H., *The Art of Counterpoint,* 2nd Ed. (Oxford University Press, 1924), p. 51. Formulas of this type do not signify modernisms at that time but just the opposite; the "classical" *cambiata* was not the point of departure but the final stage in the development.

cambiata comes to contain five notes instead of the four of the "classical"
cambiata.[26]   In the present exercises, however, we shall use only the last
named form.

Cadence formations often occur in this species with an ornamental
dissonance suspension: instead of:

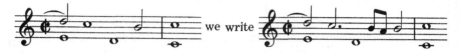

In such extended formulas it is immaterial whether the first or second
or both eighths dissonate. If eighths in general are handled melodically
according to the previously given rules,[27] they may dissonate freely.

A cadence formula which one meets, though seldom, in the music
of the sixteenth century is the following:

Here a quarter note is inserted between a suspension dissonance and
its note of resolution. It is a third below the dissonance and forms a
consonance in relation to the other voice. On the other hand, the figure
used by Fux and the theorists that followed him:

is positively not in the style of Palestrina. Undoubtedly one can find it
among the composers of the sixteenth century in rare instances; but it
is not in common use until the beginning of the eighteenth century in
composers such as Bach and Händel. Therefore Fux must have adopted
it involuntarily from his own contemporary music.

Some comments on the anticipation may likewise be in order here.
The anticipation is an unaccented quarter note which anticipates the
following accented note. From the melodic requirements for its treatment mentioned on p. 94, it follows that it is used only if it is introduced

----

[26] Some authors, for example Heinrich Schenker, assert that the classical *cambiata* forms "an
organic unit of five tones, whose succession remains invariable." (*Neue musikalische Theorien und
Phantasien,* Universal Ed., Vienna, 1910, Vol. 2, p. 308.)   Only if the fourth note of the *cambiata* is
a quarter note is it necessary to continue it to the upper second, according to the aforementioned rule
that unaccented quarter notes introduced stepwise from below must be continued by stepwise ascending movement. If the fourth note has another note value, its progression is free.
[27] Compare p. 93.

stepwise from above. In this case it is immaterial whether it dissonates or not, for example:

Particularly smooth and organic is the effect of the anticipation if it stands directly before the suspension dissonance which is decorated with eighth notes, for example:

Finally some examples of counterpoint in fifth species must be given. I emphasize again the great significance of these exercises and recommend that one spend considerable time on them. The problem involves the mastery of the harmonious relation between rest and motion, the most important problem of musical technique.

Examples

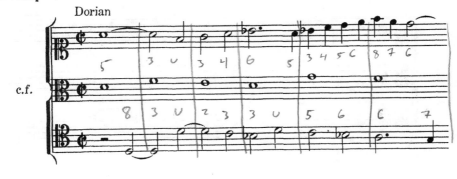

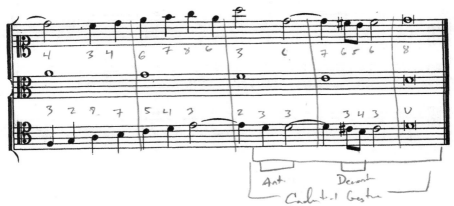

Aeolian

c.f.

Ionian

c.f.

In ternary meter, exactly the same rules apply as in binary meter.

FREE TWO-PART COUNTERPOINT

(With some comments concerning the problems of free counterpoint in three and four parts.)

For these exercises, where two free rhythmic parts are set against each other (and the cantus-firmus principle is forsaken) the same rules as for two-part fifth species are valid, for the most part. However, it is necessary to make some additions:

1. The rule that dissonance may not take place in note-against-note

has unrestricted validity only where the voices move in greater note values than quarter against quarter. On the other hand, one can find among the best composers of the sixteenth century numerous passages like the following from Palestrina's *Marcellus Mass:*

Here both of the outer parts in the first measure, second quarter, dissonate. But each voice treats its dissonance correctly in itself: the upper voice as an upward moving passing note, the lower as the classical *cambiata.* This reciprocal correctness is in general the rule in dissonant note-against-note. From time to time, also, one or more voices use dissonances with greater freedom, for example:

Palestrina: Missa Brevis

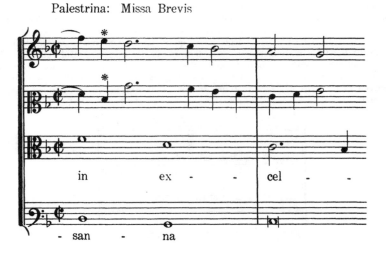

In this example the dissonance of the upper voice is certainly used as an ordinary passing dissonance, but the next to the top voice permits something so irregular as a skip of the sixth up from a dissonance which has been introduced by a skip of the third. But each voice is necessarily correctly treated in relation to the stationary voices. The rules for the dissonance treatment in "note against note" can be fomulated thus:

a. Greater note values than quarters may not dissonate with values of the same type.

b. If quarters dissonate against quarters in two-part counterpoint each voice must treat the dissonance correctly (i. e., in the same manner as when written against a cantus firmus in whole notes). This applies also to writing in three or more voices, where all the voices move in quarter against quarter.[28]

c. If in counterpoint in three or more parts, one or more voices have stationary notes, while two or more voices simultaneously move in quarter against quarter, these moving voices can make dissonances reciprocally only if each part moves correctly in relation to the stationary voices.[29]

2. The rule in accordance with which accented quarters may not be used as dissonances may be infringed in free counterpoint under the following conditions:

When four quarters, of which the first is fully accented (falls in the

---

[28] Single departures from this rule can be found even among the greatest composers of the sixteenth century, but very seldom. Compare *The Style of Palestrina*, pp. 159 f.

[29] One finds no comment concerning this subject among the earlier theorists. The first who, so far as I know, referred to it is the Englishman W. S. Rockstro. In *The Rules of Counterpoint* (London, 1882, p. 102) he writes: "These Notes (quarters) must always be irreprochable in their relations to the Bass; but notwithstanding this, they frequently make frightful collisions with each other. Now, of these collisions, the greatest of the Great Masters took no notice whatever. Provided their Florid Parts moved well with the Bass, they cared nothing for the crashes which took place between them." As evidence that this rule is insufficient, however, consider among others the following:

Here both middle voices are quite clearly correct in relation to the bass. Nevertheless this treatment is an impossibility in the style of Palestrina on account of the irregularly treated dissonance on the third quarter, which the next to the top voice introduces against the stationary D in the upper voice. It is not sufficient, therefore, that the quarter-note parts be correctly treated in relation to the bass; they must be correct in relation to all the other longer note values also, in whatever voice they may occur.

place of the first or third half note), stand together in step-wise descending motion, the third quarter, as well as the second and fourth, can dissonate. The remaining conditions for this license are the following:

    a. The fourth quarter must be followed by its upper second.[30]

    b. The counter voice must form a suspension dissonance to the quarter-note part, for example:

Figures adapt themselves for such a use especially in the cadence formula and as such were extraordinarily well-liked in the sixteenth century, both in two-part writing and in counterpoint with several parts. Particularly characteristic is the treatment in the following four-part form:

The reason the most conservative composers of Palestrina's time made frequent use of this effect, in spite of the unusually strong dissonance, is surely that they considered it a variant of the classical *cambiata,* as a kind of filled-out *cambiata.* Behind:

---

[30] This provision is important. Compare *The Style of Palestrina,* p. 112.

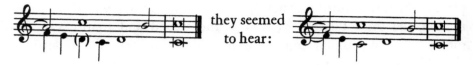

they seemed
to hear:

3. Regarding the suspension dissonance, the accompanying voice (the non-syncopating voice) does not, as in the fourth species, need to wait for the resolution of the dissonance before moving on, but can shift tones simultaneously with the syncopating voice, for example:

In such cases there are no particular restrictions on the direction of the movement in the accompanying voice except, of course, that it goes to a tone which is a consonance with the note of resolution of the dissonance, and especially that it does so in such a way that the dissonance is followed by an imperfect consonance.[31] It is also quite possible to let the accompanying voice move on before the syncope dissonance resolves; if it does, the only four possibilities for the melodic movement of the accompanying part may be grouped as follows:

  a. Either a lower or an upper auxiliary:

as used in Palestrina's mass *Viri Galilaei:*

---

[31] In such cases, "bad" suspensions such as ninths in the upper voice can be permitted when they resolve in this manner to imperfect consonances.

and in his mass *Laudate dominum:*

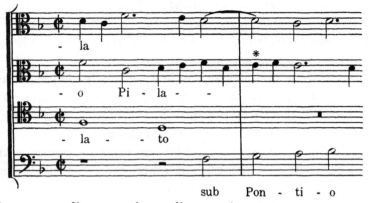

b. Or an ascending or a descending passing note:

as in Palestrina's motet *Doctor bonus:*

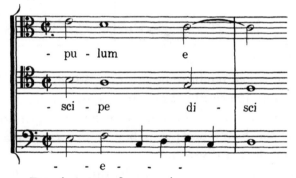

and in his motet *Domine quando veneris:*

These possibilities can be summed up in the following rule: *When the accompanying voice to the dissonant suspension moves on after only the duration of a quarter, it is necessary that* (in this voice) *the first* (accented) *quarter be followed by two steps of the second.* The only exception, merely an apparent one, is the *cambiata*.

When, as in these exercises, one writes two free melodies against each other, one must strive for an elegant and organic development of the relations between the voices not only in the horizontal but also in the vertical dimension. Thus one should, without pedantic exaggeration, take care that broad movement in any one voice is opposed with more rapid and energetic movement in the other voice, and vice versa. This is a general artistic principle to which music owes some of its greatest moments. Palestrina has mastered it as few have, for example in the mass *Spem in alium:*

Another thing which ought to be mentioned is that both voices should not syncopate simultaneously, since to do so produces a vague and unclear rhythmic effect. If the one voice has a suspension, the other ought to mark the heavy beat; it is best if this takes place in such a manner as to produce a dissonance.[32]

4. In quarter-note values, more parallel thirds and sixths may be used successively than in notes of longer value, apparently because more interesting devices (such as contrary motion) are not so effective in rapid values.

On Setting the Text

Throughout this textbook when we work without a cantus firmus we use words. Without words vocal polyphony in reality lacks its proper

---

[32] Vicentino writes concerning this: "And it will be noticed that when more than one or two parts make a suspension at the same time, the suspension does not occur in all the parts, for the suspension will not be evident; the suspension can be discerned only if at least one part sings on the beat." (*L'Antica musica . . .* , 1557, p. 33.)

foundation. For these reasons, I should like to devote some remarks to the placing of the text before we turn to the practical exercises. The rules for setting the text, as they were formulated in the sixteenth century by Vicentino and Zarlino, and as they were observed by the composers of Palestrina's day, can be summarized thus:

1. Every note value greater than a quarter note can carry a syllable.

2. A quarter note can bear a syllable only if it follows a dotted half note and is followed by a half note or a greater note value. For example:

Ky - ri - e

In this case it is preferable for each of the three notes to carry a syllable.

3. A note value which is less than a quarter cannot bear a syllable.

4. Several quarter notes which stand together can carry a single syllable of the text. For example:

- - suf - fert

5. So far as practicable, the natural utterance of the text shall be respected so that accented syllables may fall upon accented note values, and vice versa.

6. It is not good to change syllables of the text after note values less than the half note, since this makes the performance more difficult. The following placing of the text:

ful - get ec - cle - - si - - a

is acceptable, therefore, only when it is altered in such a way that the syllable *si* falls upon the last half note of the second bar. Preferably one should not shift syllables after dotted half notes (except in cases which fall in under 2). The following:

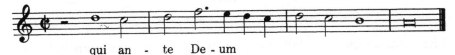

qui an - te De - um

is entirely satisfactory only if the syllable *um* is placed under the last note.

7. It is natural that the final syllable should coincide with the final tone in the musical phrase. Out of regard for this one will often tolerate forms such as:

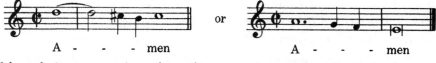

A - - - men   or   A - - - men

although it goes against the rule set up in number 6. It is, however, especially in the cadences that one can find these and similar licenses in the composers of the sixteenth century.

8. In imitation, the setting of the text at the first appearance of the theme must be maintained without change in all subsequent entries.

9. Repetition of tones requires new syllables of the text, with the exception of tonal entries that have ornamental character (as with the anticipation).

Practical Exercise

Write some short compositions with two free voices to texts like: *Kyrie eleison, Amen, Alleluia* or similar ones. *Kyrie,* according to Palestrina's practice, may be divided into two or three syllables. The best results will generally be obtained if both voices are written simultaneously; if one voice is composed first and then the other their merit may easily be unequal. (This advice applies to all polyphonic composition.) Unison may be used freely, of course, but with caution. Repetition of tones is allowed when it is motivated by the text (compare 9 above). In the case of "dead" intervals (intervals which are found between the final note in one melodic phrase and the initial tone of the next and which are made clear by textual separation), occasionally forbidden intervals can be used, such as the descending sixth, the major sixth, and sevenths. The following example is from the Credo of Palestrina's *Marcellus Mass:*

A - - - - men, A - - - -

I have constructed the following examples on motives from Palestrina, since it is difficult to find longer two-part episodes without imitation in Palestrina or other composers from the period.

Examples

---

[33] In free counterpoint, where there are so many opportunities for variation, it is not necessary, especially in middle or lower voices, to observe the culmination note principle so strictly.

IMITATION

Imitation in music means a manner of writing in which one voice imitates or mimics the other, taking over the theme of the other, so that the voices enter in succession each having the same melodic material.

Imitation is one of the means best suited to the polyphonic style. This may seem strange, since it appears to be contrary to the principle of polyphony, in that the independence of the voices is apparently restricted, all the voices being limited to the same theme. One must take into consideration, however, that "melodic independence" can be obtained only with considerable difficulty when the rhythmic movement of the parts is equal.

On the other hand, imitation, at least in every case when it is based upon a characteristic theme, is always effective and gives the impression of rich musical life and vigorous mental activity. Through imitation the voices in polyphonic writing are woven together so that compositions in this style attain a stronger feeling of unity in spite of all individuality and contrast in the diverse voices. From this fundamental approach to the universal aesthetic requirement of antiquity, "unity in variety," imitative style has gained its enormous vitality and enduring validity.

Imitation may be divided into several different kinds: strict, free, tonal, and real. Strict imitation means an imitation in which the intervals of the theme are followed exactly, while free imitation allows, for example, a major interval to be answered by a minor one of the same kind, or permits other slight modifications of the theme. Tonal imitation means imitation in which particular attention is given to the establishment and maintenance of the tonality; for example, the tonic is clearly answered with the dominant, and vice versa. If the imitation is not tonal, it is called real. Tonal imitation was especially popular in the seventeenth and eighteenth centuries. With Bach and Händel, tonal imitation was the usual procedure.

In the sixteenth century, on the other hand, the real answer to a subject was preferred: for example, the beginning of Palestrina's four-part motet *Hodie beata:*

This excerpt is in the Dorian mode transposed to G. One will observe that the theme, as given by the bass and alto, skips tonic to dominant, G–D, while the tenor and soprano answer with D–A. A tonal answer would have required: dominant-tonic, D–G. As has been said, the "real" answer is the most common in the Palestrina period; one can, however, occasionally come upon tonal imitation; for example, at the beginning of Palestrina's four-part motet *Surge propera,* whose theme was cited earlier:

Sur - ge, pro - pe - ra a - mi - ca me - a, a - mi - ca me -

Sur - - ge, pro - pe - ra a - mi - ca

Sur - -

- - a, a - mi - ca me - a,

me - - a, a - mi - ca me - a, sur - ge pro - pe -

ge, pro - pe - ra a - mi - ca me - a, a - mi - ca me - a, a -

Sur - - ge, pro - pe -

In addition to the manners already mentioned, imitation can further-more take place by "inversion." This means that the intervals of the theme are answered in contrary motion: skip of the fifth up by skip of the fifth down, and so on. For example:

Ky - rie e - lei - - -

Ky - rie e - lei - - - son,

Answers may furthermore be formed by "augmentation" or by "diminution" where all the following voices double or halve the original
time values of the motive.   The following example illustrates an answer
by augmentation:

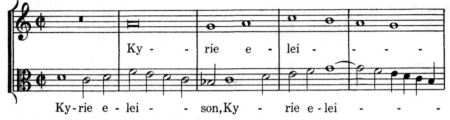

and the next an answer *per diminutionem:*

A famous example of diminution is in Palestrina's four-part *Missa
Brevis:*

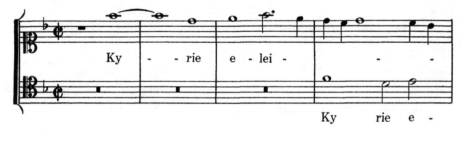

Among the composers of Palestrina's time, a relatively sparing use
was made of imitation by inversion, augmentation, or diminution.   In

the earlier part of the sixteenth century, the time of the Netherland composers, and also in the following century, these procedures were used more
frequently in polyphonic composition.

During the height of the polyphonic period a similar, more artistic kind
of imitation was commonly used: namely, the *"stretto."* The *stretto*
is a form of imitation in which the following voices enter with the theme
before the preceding voice has reached the end, as in Palestrina's motet
Fuit homo:

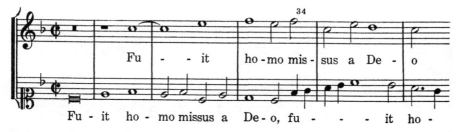

The motive extends here over three and three-quarters bars; nevertheless
the upper voice enters after only one and a half bars of rest. Note that
while (as always in the last part of the sixteenth century) the theme
begins with a full measure, it is answered by the following voice on the
third beat in the bar. Such rhythmic modifications are extraordinarily
common in composers of Palestrina's time, even when the relation of
the accents in the theme is thereby so completely altered that accented notes
become unaccented, and vice versa.[35]

Imitation may occur in any interval relationship whatsoever. That
is, the imitation can begin on any degree of the scale. Likewise one can
begin with any consonance, perfect or imperfect, or with any note that
produces a permissible syncope dissonance.

But in the Palestrina style itself, imitation in the fifth is by far the
most common. Also imitations in the unison and the octave are often
used, especially in choruses of the same voices; on the other hand, imitations on other intervals occur only occasionally, for the most part in connection with artistic canonic developments.

It is important in imitation to choose motives that are effective. Especially with longer imitations it is dangerous to make melodies too smooth
with constant use of stepwise movement or very small intervals; in such

---

[34] The hidden octave is explained by the imitation.
[35] See the quotation from Vicentino, pp. 21 f.

cases the imitations easily elude the listener. Here it would be desirable
to have a slightly abrupt movement, a large, striking interval, or the
like, of course within the melodic rules of the style. Notice how beautiful and nobly effective the upward skip of the octave is in Palestrina's
motet *O quantus luctus*. Besides the expressive treatment of the text,
the strong emphasis placed on the word *"quantus"* through the octave skip
is doubtless for expressive purposes. The purely musical requirements
are fulfilled with extraordinary mastery.

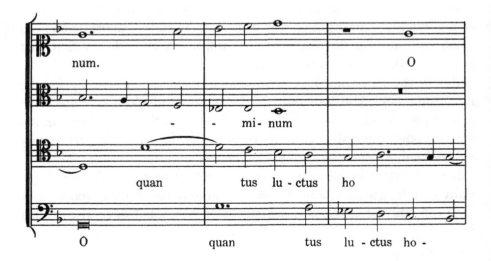

Two other singularly beautiful examples of imitation from the works of Palestrina follow:

The upper voice in the last example has already been cited as a type of Palestrina melody in its most beautiful form. It may seem incredible that its effect could be enhanced in any way. Nevertheless the effect is enhanced in the two-part imitative form. In all points the lower voice supports and strengthens the effect. It is as though one met, in these two voices, eye-witnesses to a divine miracle who now unite into one entranced witness. This inspired example reveals the hand of a genius in every detail.

Practical Exercise

Write some two-part Kyries with imitation. Since such compact two-part compositions are not to be found in Palestrina's compositions (Palestrina seems never to have written for less than three voices), and since other two-part compositions from the time of Palestrina are generally too extensive to be used as models here, I have provided examples, some based on Gregorian motives and some on motives taken from Palestrina. It may be remarked that the imitating voice is not obliged to introduce more of the theme than the preceding voice has sung at the entrance of the imitation and that it is permissible to let the second voice begin with an imperfect consonance.

Examples

---

[36] It should be observed here that in the "polyphonic" Phrygian mode in imitation B (not C as in the Gregorian music) is regarded as the dominant. See the footnote, p. 71.

Mixolydian

In ternary meters exactly the same rules apply as in binary, for example:

Ionian

A valuable exercise is to attempt to write imitations to the same theme at every interval, a procedure used by composers in the time of Palestrina when they applied themselves to especially artistic forms of imitation. The following may serve as models:

Imitation at the unison, Phrygian

Imitation at the second, Dorian

Imitation at the third, Aeolian

Imitation at the fourth, Dorian

Imitation at the fifth, Aeolian

Imitation at the sixth, Ionian

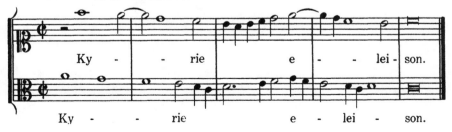

Imitation at the seventh, Mixolydian

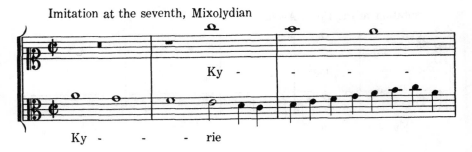

Chapter IV

THREE-PART COUNTERPOINT

FIRST SPECIES

IN THREE-PART counterpoint, for the first time it is possible to use a chord consisting of root, third, and fifth—a fundamental concept which in harmony is called a triad. In this and the following problems, we should seek to introduce as many complete triads as may be compatible with good voice leading, which in the last analysis is more important. Furthermore, in three-part counterpoint, which is less "transparent" than two-part, we can take certain liberties with regard to the rules given in two-part counterpoint:

1. Perfect and augmented fourths, diminished fifths, and (more exceptionally) diminished fourths can be considered and treated as consonant combinations, but only when they do not occur in relation to the bass. All dissonances are heard most clearly in relation to the bass and hence weaker dissonances, like those mentioned above, are allowed when they are put between the upper and middle voices or between two middle voices. In other words, in three-part writing we can use triads in root position and chords of the sixth, for example:

On the other hand, six-four chords must be handled as dissonant

chords, since they involve a fourth relation to the bass:[1] One

---

[1] Translator's note. For a more comprehensive discussion of the six-four chord, see Haydon, Glen: *The Evolution of the Six-Four Chord.* Berkeley, University of California Press, 1933.

can likewise permit the free use of the diminished triad as a chord of

the sixth (but only as such), for example: and indeed

also the augmented triad in first inversion, which, although rare, does
occur in Palestrina, for example in the mass *Salvum fac:*

2.   The rule that no one of two voices that skip in similar motion may
make a skip greater than a fourth (not counting the octave) is valid,
in counterpoint in three and more parts, only when outer voices are concerned and even then only where all voices move in similar motion.

3.   Concealed fifths or octaves are permitted between an outer voice
and an inner voice or between inner voices (when there are more than
three parts).   Between outer voices, hidden fifths can be used with good
effect, but in this case the upper part should move in conjunct motion.
Hidden octaves between outer voices (at least in less than four parts)
ought to be avoided.   They may occur in cadences at the progression
from the next to the last to the last measure; but otherwise they must
be used with caution.

4.   Unisons can be used freely between two voices, but all three voices
can strike the unison only in the first or last bar of the exercise.

5.   One can begin and end with the complete triad, but only with the
tonic triad.   In such a case the beginning chord ought to have a major
third; yet only if, as in first species, all voices begin together.   If, on

the other hand, the thirds enter after the cantus firmus, they can very well be minor. In the final chord, the third should under all circumstances be major. Besides closing with the complete triad, one can end with a "triad" with omitted third or fifth. But, on the other hand, one can begin only with a complete or "empty" triad (with third omitted).

6. Leading tones may not be doubled: C-sharp in Dorian, F in Phrygian, F-sharp in Mixolydian, G-sharp in Aeolian, and B in Ionian.

Practical Exercise

Set two parts in whole notes to the cantus firmus. The cantus firmus can be treated in three ways: as upper, lower, or middle part.

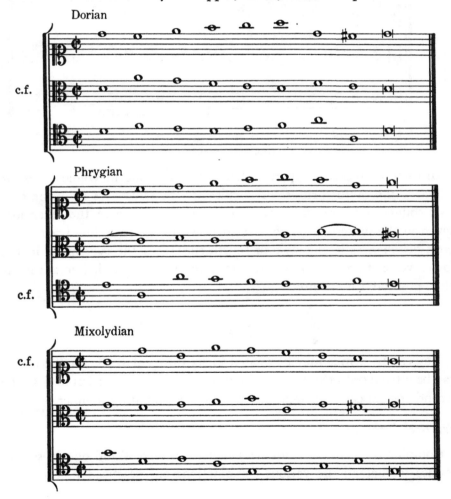

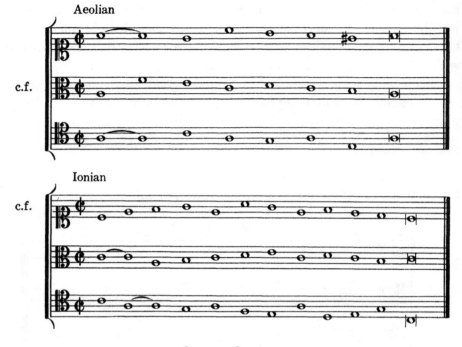

SECOND SPECIES

In these exercises, one part in half notes and one in whole notes are added to the cantus firmus. The rules are the same here as in the two-part counterpoint, second species, with the exception of the extensions given in the preceding section. Cadences may be introduced with syncope dissonances in the style of fourth species; if the syncope is in the lower voice it may be resolved into a diminished triad, but always in close position, for example:

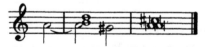

The cantus firmus may be treated in six different ways, for the cantus can be introduced in any one of the three voices, and the parts in first and second species can exchange places in a corresponding manner.

Practical Exercise

Combine the cantus firmus with one voice in first and one in second species so that all the various combinations are practiced in turn:

Dorian

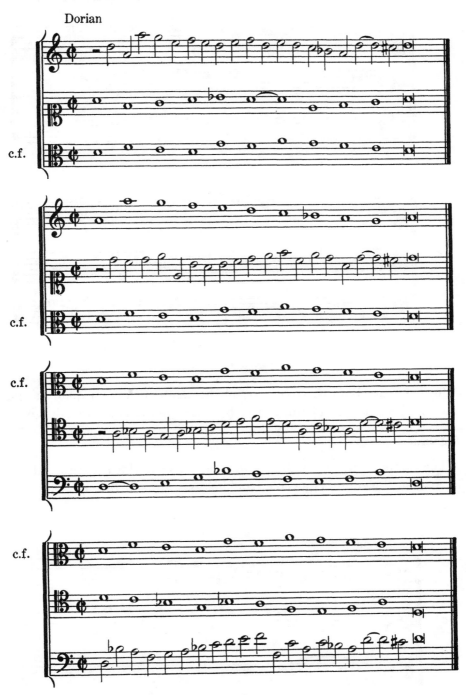

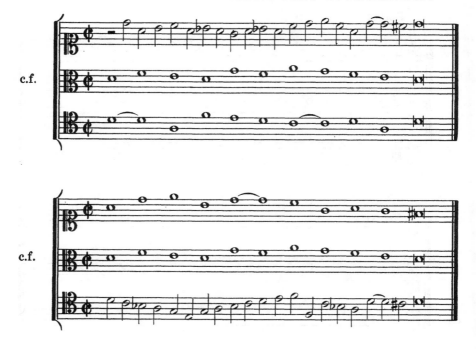

c.f.

c.f.

THIRD SPECIES

In these exercises one voice is set to the cantus firmus in quarters and one in whole notes. Nothing is to be added to the rules already given.

Practical Exercise

The cantus firmus is combined with one voice in third species and one in first, so that the six possible combinations are run through one after the other.

Dorian

c.f.

Mixolydian

c.f.

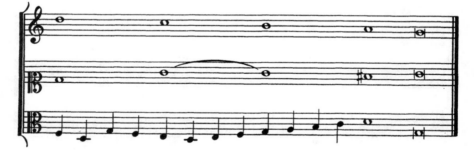

Aeolian

c.f.

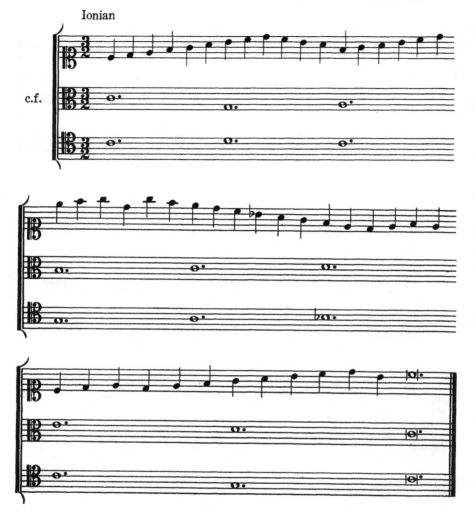

A profitable but difficult exercise is to try to set the cantus firmus with
a part in second species and a part in third species. The difficulties consist especially in making the second species logical and flowing. When
it comes against a part in quarters, one listens in terms of the four quarters, and the second half note (third quarter) is felt, therefore, as accented
and cannot dissonate. The problem is especially difficult when the second species lies in the lower voice. If, on the other hand, it lies in the
middle or upper voice, one may use fourths (naturally legitimized by
having the third or fifth below), and possibilities for stepwise movement
are thereby increased. At the cadence it is permissible to let the part in

second species introduce a dissonant suspension according to the rules of fourth species. In such cases such freer forms as the following may be used:

To be sure, the upper voice skips to the dissonance and leaves it with a skip; but one is inclined to overlook irregularities because the upper part skips down to the E in the middle voice (which is correctly treated in relation to the dissonance) and immediately skips back to the tone from which it came, and to consider it as if it were:

Such dissonances occur when a part, actually incorrect in itself in one or more points, coincides with and hides behind a more correctly treated voice which is more prominent. These "parasitic" or "covered" dissonances are not rare among sixteenth century composers.[2] The following characteristic case is taken from Palestrina's canticum *Nunc dimittis*.

Here the skip in the first tenor from D to G, which is actually incorrect (dissonating with C in the upper voice), is made possible by the fact that the G of the tenor is in unison with the G of the bass, and thus is correct

---

[2] Compare *The Style of Palestrina*, p. 156.

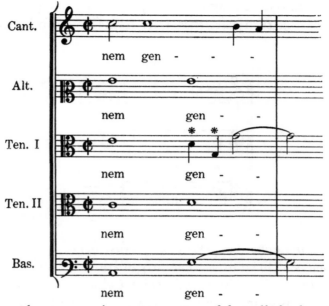

nem gen - - -

in relation to the upper voices; as a matter of fact all the last three tones in the tenor are found in the other voices.

Examples

FOURTH SPECIES

In this species a part in the fourth and a part in first species are added to the cantus firmus. Here the rules are the same as for the two-part fourth species, but with certain extensions. Thus "bad" dissonant suspensions such as fourths and sevenths in the lower voice, or seconds or ninths in the upper voices, may be used if in any such case a "good" suspension is produced at the same time in relation to another part:

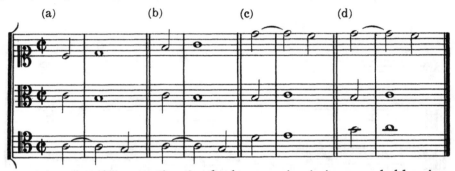

In (a) a fourth suspension in the lower voice is irreproachable, since the voice at the same time forms a dissonance of the second with the B in the middle voice. In (b) a seventh suspension is acceptable in the lower voice for the same reason. Likewise (c) and (d) contain a seventh and a fourth suspension, respectively, making the suspended ninth between the upper voices acceptable.

Practical Exercise

Set each cantus firmus in the various combinations. The "consonant fourth" used in the Aeolian example is discussed pp. 193 ff.

Dorian

Phrygian

Mixolydian

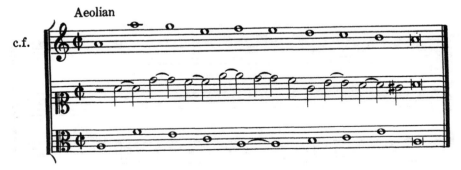

Aeolian

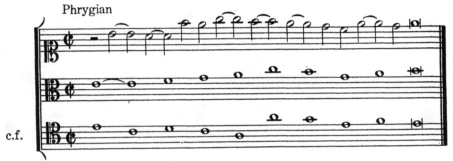

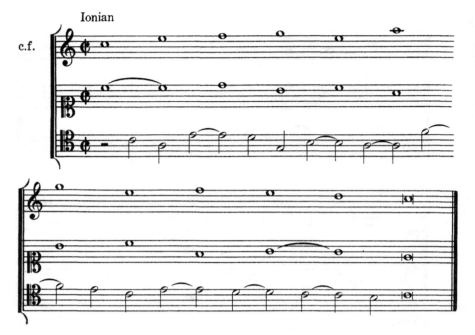

A valuable exercise is to combine third and fourth species:

---

[3] Compare the rules, p. 158.

Dorian

Phrygian

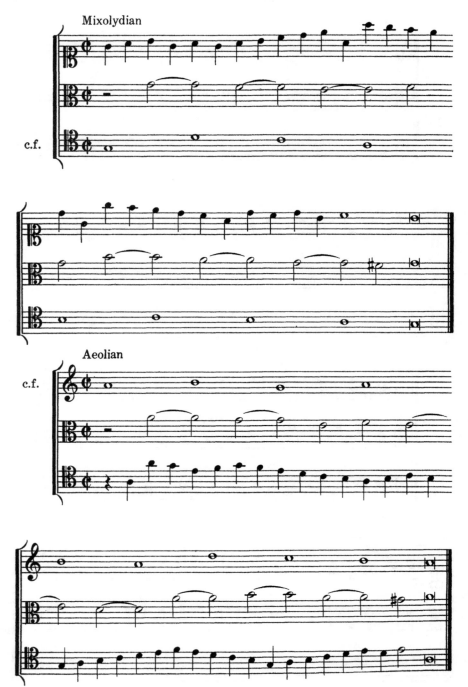

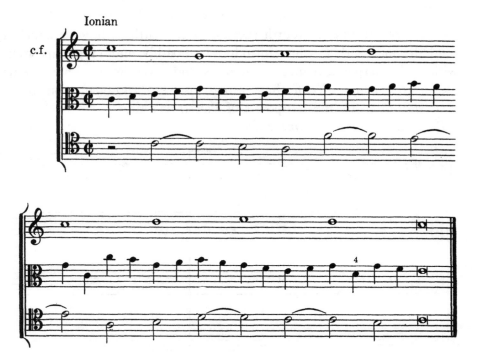

FIFTH SPECIES

The same rules apply here, as in two-part writing in the same species, as well as the mitigating qualifications just stated as applying generally in three-part writing.

Here the concept "consonant fourth" must be mentioned. The so-called "consonant fourth" is a fourth brought in stepwise upon the thesis (weak beat) over a stationary bass tone. Thereafter it is tied over to the next following arsis (strong beat), where it is changed into a stronger dissonance; but finally manages to make its regular resolution upon the next thesis (weak beat), for example:

---

4 The D of the middle part is covered by its octave relation to the upper part.

Thus a suspension is introduced, prepared by a dissonance, logically in violation of the rules of fourth species. The fourth is, however, such a mild dissonance that, when introduced smoothly and in juxtaposition with such sharp dissonances as seconds and sevenths, it almost seems like a consonance. With these provisions, the "consonant fourth" is used very often by the composers of Palestrina's time.

Palestrina.   Mass: *L'homme armé*

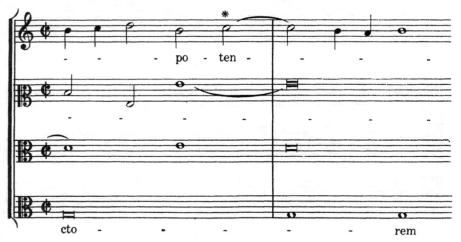

Examples

This idiom was used in the counterpoint written against the fifth and sixth notes of the Aeolian cantus firmus at the bottom of page 189.

Dorian

c.f.

Free writing without imitation is unusual but worth trying:

IMITATION

Two-part imitation is written to the cantus firmus. Exercises of this type are most profitable and are therefore especially recommended, for example:

Concerning imitation in three free parts, nothing is to be added to the rules already given.

One should try to use the most complete harmonies possible. An especially beautiful effect is obtained if the third voice enters in such a way that it supplements the other voices to produce a complete triad. If the third part enters at a suspension dissonance as in bar 7 of the following Benedictus from Palestrina's *Missa Brevis,* the charm of the effect is enhanced even more. I should like to give this Benedictus here in its entirety, as an especially beautiful model for three-part imitative writing. One should study the perfect suitability of both these themes for this form of treatment—a thing which is very rare.

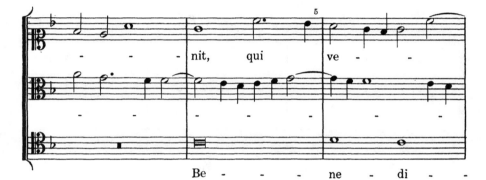

[5] Irregular setting of the text.

Do - mi - ni, Do - mi

ne, in - no - mi - ne

- - - - mi - ni,

ni, in no - mi - ne

in no - mi - ne

in no - mi - ne Do - - - - mi -

Do - - - - mi - ni.

Do - - mi - ni, Do - mi - ni.

ni, in no - mi - ne Do - mi - ni.

Chapter V

FOUR-PART COUNTERPOINT

First Species

THE FOLLOWING rule is to be added to the ones already given: Covered octaves are admissible, but they had best be used when the upper part moves by step.

Examples

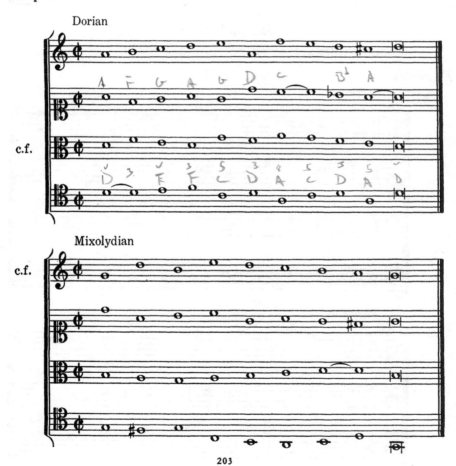

Ionian

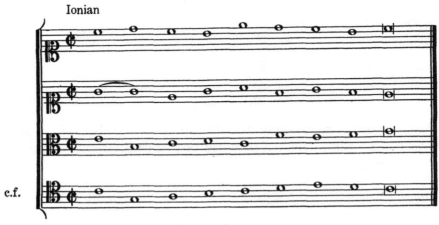

c.f.

SECOND SPECIES

No additional rules are necessary.

Examples

Dorian

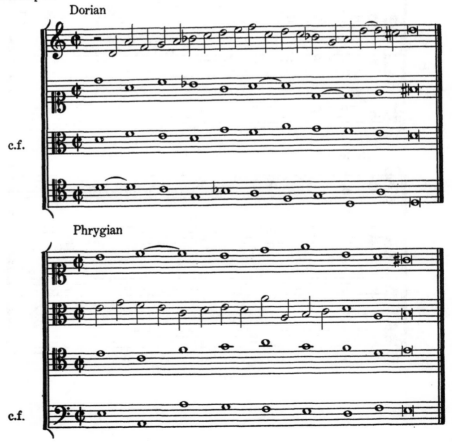

c.f.

Phrygian

c.f.

Mixolydian

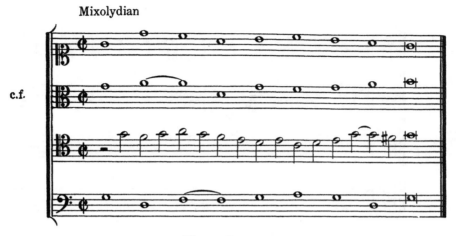

c.f.

THIRD SPECIES

Examples

Dorian

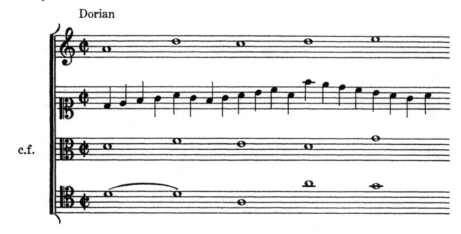

c.f.

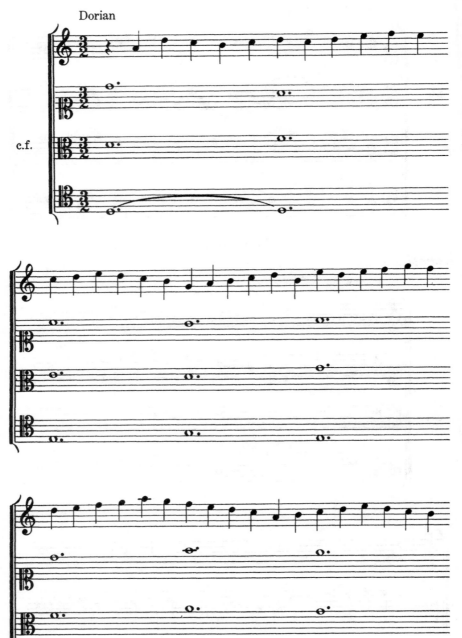

Aeolian

c.f.

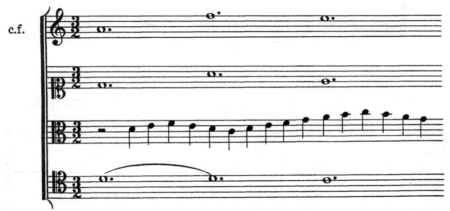

A very difficult exercise but one that is most instructive is to add one part each in the first, second, and third species to the cantus firmus. For example:

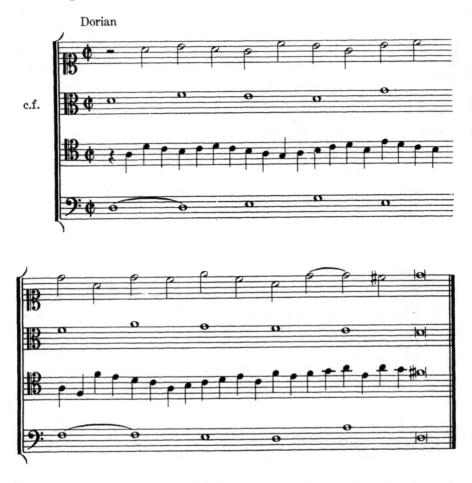

Dorian

c.f.

Notice that the unaccented half notes are all consonant against the moving quarters. See the comment on page 184.

FOURTH SPECIES

One part is added to the cantus firmus in syncopes, and the two other added parts are in whole notes. For example:

Dorian

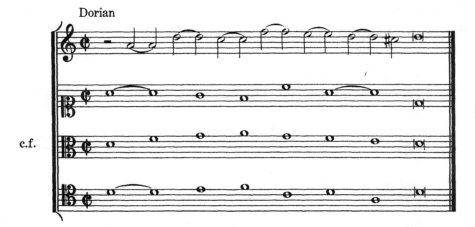

c.f.

The attempt to write one part each in the fourth, second, and first species against the given cantus firmus is a very useful exercise. The unaccented half notes of the counterpoint in the second species may be passing dissonances; and of course the accented half notes of the part in fourth species may be dissonances. For example:

c.f.

But probably the most difficult exercise of all in the study of counterpoint is to add to the cantus firmus one part each in the second, third, and fourth species, so that each of the four strict species is represented in the same exercise. It may seem almost impossible to observe simultaneously all the requirements, both melodic and harmonic; yet with a little practice it can be done, and time devoted to exercises of this type will be most profitably spent. These exercises are excellent for teaching the art of the individualization of the separate parts under even the most difficult circumstances. Several examples follow:

Dorian

c.f.

Dorian

c.f.

Mixolydian

c.f.

FIFTH SPECIES

One free part, according to the rules for fifth species, and two parts in first species are written against the cantus firmus:

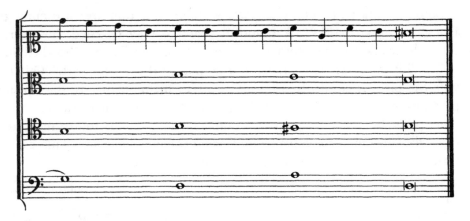

Ionian

c.f.

Compositions with four free parts without imitation are rare among Palestrina's own works. A beautiful example may be cited, however, from the works of the Roman composer Costanzo Festa, who died in 1545. But even here there is some imitation in the second part. Otherwise the piece is constructed on a Gregorian melody; that is, the upper part introduces a Gregorian melody almost note for note, though the other parts show no relation to this cantus firmus. In the fourth measure from the end an incorrectly treated *cambiata* is noticeable. This early form was no longer in use in the real Palestrina period.[1]

Costanzo Festa[2]

1 See *The Style of Palestrina*, p. 195.
2 This composition is given here in accordance with codex 21 of the Vatican chapel archives.

IMITATION

An exercise which is not easy but nevertheless instructive is the addition of three parts in imitation, for example:

Four-part compositions with imitation in all voices are most common in the sixteenth century. From a countless number of examples I have selected one of the most beautiful, the beginning of the four-part motet *Ego sum panis* by Palestrina. This composition is in the Ionian mode transposed to F. The soprano begins with the dominant of the scale and the other parts follow, entering alternately on the tonic and dominant with strict regularity. Moreover, the effective entrance of the parts is remarkable; one never feels that the entrance of a voice is superfluous or

pointless. The entrance of the tenor is particularly effective, coming as
it does on a suspended dissonance in accordance with a favorite procedure
of Palestrina and his contemporaries. The tenor seems to gather all the
reins into his hand, for with the entrance of the tenor voice one realizes
at once that the somewhat indefinite, vaguely undulating beginning is
merely the gentle introduction of a musical structure of unusual strength
and solidity:

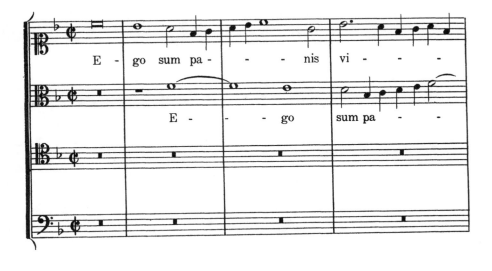

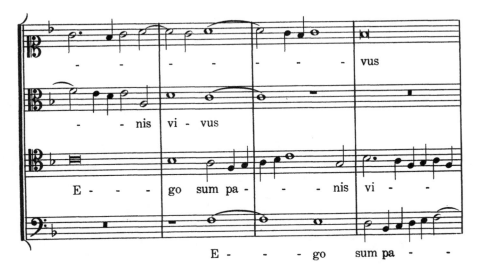

Chapter VI

COUNTERPOINT IN MORE THAN FOUR PARTS

IN German a composition which has more than four parts is called *"vielstimmig."* [1] Though about 1500 most musical compositions were written for four voices, in the course of the sixteenth century the situation gradually changed so that by the time of Palestrina compositions in more than four parts greatly predominated. A difference between the normal style of polyphonic writing in the sixteenth century and that in the seventeenth and eighteenth centuries is that the independence of the several voices strictly maintained in the earlier period frequently gives way to the doubling of one part with another in the later period, so that the polyphony of the composition is somewhat illusory. As Bellermann says: [2]

> The great composers of the sixteenth century always proceed very strictly in this matter. In their polyphonic works every single voice, regardless of how many there may be in all, was considered an independent being whose individuality should not and could not be confused with another. By carrying out the principle of polyphonic composition in this logical manner, they attained that remarkable harmony of sound, that mighty development of the tonal mass which obtains when the various voices enter one by one, in a word those tonal effects which the composers of later times seek in vain.

The treatment of counterpoint in more than four parts follows essentially the rules for four-part writing, but naturally the more voices the composition contains, the greater the requirement for complete harmonies. On the other hand, the multi-part treatment affords greater freedom in the use of hidden parallels in that covered octaves are permitted between outer parts even if the upper part moves by skip. In writing in five or

---

[1] Translator's note. The translator does not know of an English word in current use that is the exact equivalent of *"vielstimmig."* Literally, it means "many voiced."

[2] *Der Kontrapunkt*, Fourth Edition, p. 420.

more parts it is necessary to double one or more of the voice types; that is, there will be two altos, two tenors, and so on. The more the parts in a composition, the greater the difficulties in working out a tonally rich theme. Thus we observe that composers of the sixteenth century make constantly increasing use of tonal repetition in their works, especially in seven- and eight-part writing. And the voice leading, too, becomes increasingly difficult as the number of voices grows. In sixteenth century compositions of six or more parts the simultaneous use of all the voices is, as a rule, only for periods of short duration.

The following example of five-part writing is by the Belgian composer Jacob de Kerle, a contemporary of Palestrina (*ca.* 1531–1591), who spent a large part of his life in Italy. The composition is refined and shows ability even if, as an early work of this master, it may now and then seem somewhat old-fashioned as compared with the mature works of Palestrina: [3]

Jacob de Kerle

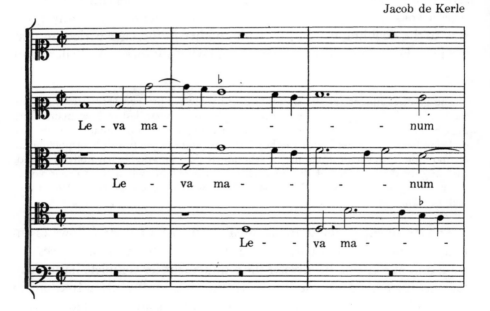

---

[3] The composition is taken from Otto Ursprung's edition of the selected works of J. de Kerle, in *Denkmäler der Tonkunst in Bayern,* 26th year.

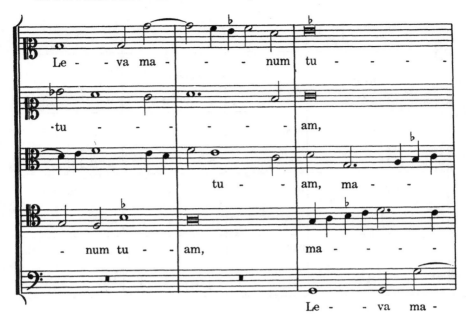

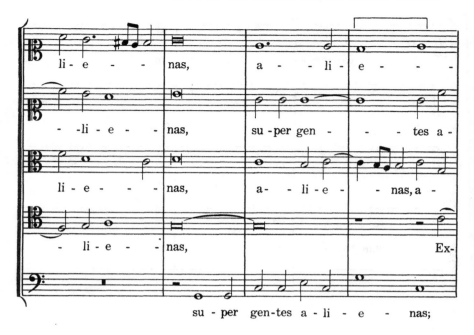

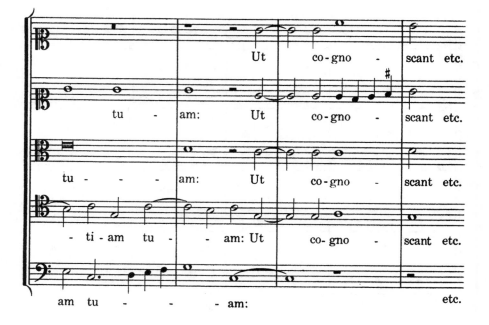

In six-part compositions the choir is often divided into two three-part groups or into one four-part and one two-part tonal group, and the like. These choirs then answer each other, at times, and at times unite. Among others, Palestrina's six-part motet *Viri Galilaei* affords an excellent model for this technique. The composition is written for two sopranos, one alto, two tenors, and a bass. The first soprano and the alto begin with the exclamation *"Viri Galilaei,"* which is then repeated by a five-part choir consisting of sopranos, tenors, and the bass. The alto and the men's voices continue with *"quid statis,"* the women's (more accurately, the boys') voices with the second tenor repeat this, and only at the significant words *"Hic Jesus"* do all the parts enter together:

Palestrina uses a very different technique, one based less upon tonal effects, in his seven-part motet *Tu es Petrus*. Here alto, tenor, and bass are doubled, and the themes which are not particularly adapted to polyphonic treatment are worked out beautifully and with apparent ease. It is worth noting that the composition does not actually become seven-

part until toward the end (not included in the portion given here). By having at least one part always at rest, the treatment is sufficiently flexible for the imitative character of the writing to be maintained without the slightest difficulty.

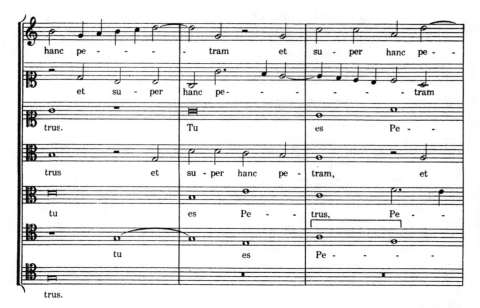

Eight-part writing in the sixteenth century is almost always treated like dual four-part composition, that is, in double chorus style. This type of composition, which seems to have come originally from Venice, during the century spread to the Roman school and gradually became common throughout all Europe. As a rule, however, the individuality of the two choruses is not strictly maintained. Thus the higher voices of one choir are often combined with lower voices of another, and in general nearly every tonal possibility is employed with a genuinely refined feeling for the color effect. Even eight-part writing requires—in general at least—a more harmonic-homophonic style of treatment; with still more parts the working out of themes that are largely stepwise in their melodic structure becomes almost impossible. The voice leading is likewise easily weakened by the frequent exchange of tones to which one must here turn as a last resort. ("Exchange of tones" means that two or more voices interchange tones, for example: .)

Palestrina is able, however, even in eight-part writing to preserve the basic polyphonic character of the style. His superior mastery of this type of composition may be illustrated by the beginning of his motet *Laudate Dominum:*

Chapter VII

THE CANON

A CANON IS A COMPOSITION based on imitation in which all voices have exactly the same melodic content, so that the part which begins the composition is copied or imitated note for note in each of the other parts. A difference between ordinary imitation and the canon is that in the former only the beginning (the theme) is taken from the voice which immediately precedes, whereas in the latter the whole melodic structure of this voice is taken over either by simple repetition or by transposition to another pitch.

The canon is the oldest of all imitative forms. It is to be found as early as the thirteenth century, and in the music of the fourteenth century, the so-called *ars nova,* it was frequently used by French and even more often by Italian composers. In Italy it was given the characteristic name *caccia* (hunt), but in the fifteenth and sixteenth centuries it was generally called *fuga* (flight). Relatively early, however, the latter term was used for another contrapuntal form, and the canon was given its present name. Towards the end of the fifteenth century and the beginning of the sixteenth, the canon form had its period of florescence, especially among the Netherland composers. Here it appeared as a rule as a "riddle canon"; the composer noted only the principal voice and added some sentence from which one can puzzle out the nature and character of the voices to be derived from it. For example, the statement "He who follows me will not walk in darkness" means that in the execution of the canonic part the black notes of the written part are simply to be skipped. In the first half of the sixteenth century people began to tire of these often artistically specious tricks, and with the music of Palestrina the most brilliant period of the canon was passed. Palestrina himself did write one four-part *Missa ad fugam,* in which only two parts are written out; the other two parts simply imitate the first two canonically and are therefore not written out.   But this composition is a work of his youth, and later Palestrina seems not to have written any exclusively canonic composition.   On the other hand, he used canonic writing frequently in combination with other voices using free imitation, especially in the Kyrie and in the Agnus Dei of a number of masses.

The procedure in writing a canon is quite simple.   One voice begins, and then the same succession of intervals is taken up by one or more voices in succession while the first voice or the preceding voices continue with counterpoint.   This counterpoint is then introduced in the following voice or voices, and so on.   If a canon is to be concluded in polyphonic style, it must be broken off with a cadence.   The following canon is interrupted in next to the last measure:

In the foregoing canon the imitation is in the fifth, but, just as in ordinary imitation, it can take place at any desired interval.   *Cancrizans* is the name given to a type of canon in which the melodic structure of the initial voice is imitated by retrogression: the following voice repeats the melody backwards.

Canon "by augmentation" (*per augmentationem*) is the name given a type of canon in which the note values of the leading voice are doubled in the following voice as opposed to the canon "by diminution" (*per diminutionem*), in which the corresponding note values are reduced by one half.   With the exception of the last two forms, none of these types of canons, however, has any great musical value.

A canon combined with free imitative voices is given below—a Kyrie
from Palestrina's five-part mass *Repleatur os meum laude*. All voices
begin with the same theme, but a canonical relation develops only between the second soprano and the tenor, when the higher part makes a
canon in the octave to the lower:

Chapter VIII

THE MOTET

BESIDES THE MASS, the motet is the chief form in the religious music of the sixteenth century. The term *motet*, of which the origin is uncertain, dates from the twelfth and thirteenth centuries, when it referred to one of the contrapuntal voices added to the cantus firmus of a polyphonic composition. Later the name was transferred to the composition itself, at first if a sacred text was used, but later also if the text was secular or even if one voice sang a sacred text while another sang a secular text. That is, in the middle ages the concept of the motet implied that the different voices should simultaneously sing different texts. In the fifteenth and sixteenth centuries motets meant exclusively compositions with the sacred Latin texts which then, as a rule, were used for all voices. The words, in most cases, are taken from the Latin translation of the Bible (the Vulgate), but occasionally independent religious poems were used.

Characteristic of the musical treatment of the motet is that each line or division of the text has its independent theme, generally imitated more or less strictly in all voices before the next portion of the text and the corresponding theme are introduced. The motet thereby becomes an aggregation of different imitations or of more homophonic episodes. One of the chief difficulties in the formal treatment of this type of composition, therefore, is to prevent all these fragments from merely forming a mosaic-like structure made up of a disjointed series of sections, and to unite them into an organic whole. Palestrina's Netherland predecessors often seem somewhat angular and inelastic in this respect; Palestrina himself and his contemporaries, on the other hand, understood to a rare degree the art of constructing transitions.

The Palestrina four-part motet *Dies sanctificatus* will serve as an ex-

ample of this form of composition.   It is intended for the Christmas mass
and is filled with exultant, pious joy.   The mode is Mixolydian:

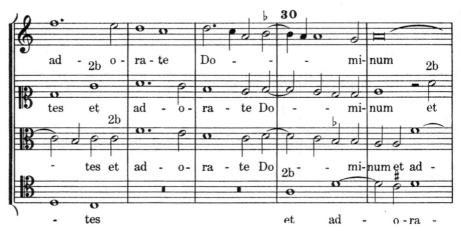

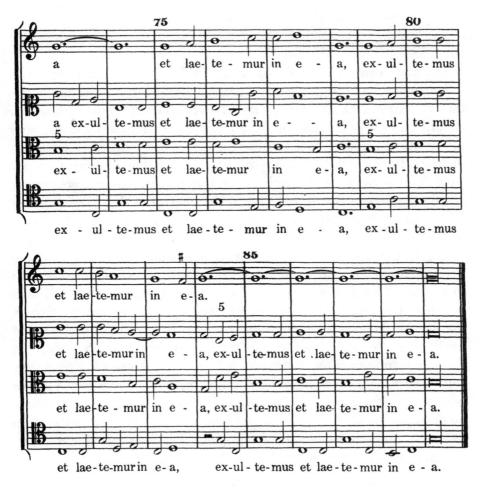

From the viewpoint of technical musical construction, the composition falls into five smaller sections:

1. *Dies sanctificatus illuxit nobis,*
2. *venite, gentes, et adorate Dominum,*
3. *quia hodie descendit lux magna in terris;*
4. *haec dies quam fecit Dominus:*
5. *exultemus et laetemur in ea.*

A literal translation would read as follows:

1. A holy day has dawned upon us,
2. Come ye people and worship the Lord,

3. For today a great light has descended upon the earth;
4. This is the day which the Lord hath made;
5. Let us rejoice and be glad in it.

The first theme consists of two parts: (*a*) "*Dies sanctificatus,*" and (*b*)
"*illuxit nobis,*" and begins in the soprano. In the second measure of the
theme, however, the alto enters with an exact imitation in the fifth below.
As often in his other compositions, Palestrina here makes the first and
introductory period a canonic duet in accordance with Netherlandian
models. In the eighth measure the tenor enters with the theme, a bar
later the bass enters on the fifth below, and the two lower voices repeat
exactly the duet of the upper voices at the interval of the octave. Meanwhile the soprano and alto continue in free counterpoint to the lower
parts. This principle of construction, too, is decidedly Netherlandian.
In bar 12 the second part of the theme is separated from the first and
developed independently, and at bar 17 the first part of the motet comes
to an end. Now follows a new part of the text (*venite gentes*) and with
it a new theme that, after two and a half measures, is imitated first in
the alto (in the unison), then in the tenor (in the unison in *stretto*), and
finally after two more measures in the soprano and bass, the former in
the octave and the latter in the fifth below with the up-beat lengthened,
and this development is thereby brought to an end. The work continues
with the words "*et adorate Dominum.*" The theme 2*b,* which is sung
by the soprano, has no really independent character, but is developed out
of and in connection with the counterpoint which is introduced in the
alto immediately before over the last "*venite*" of the tenor:

ve - ni - te   gen - - - tes

This theme is imitated exactly only once, in the tenor (in the octave)
beginning at the end of the following measure. The remaining imitative entrances merely suggest the theme somewhat vaguely, chiefly
through rhythmic similarity. The technical structure of this episode
can be thought of only as a sort of hybrid between polyphonic and homophonic writing. Chordal considerations predominate. It is primarily a
descending series of chords of the sixth. As has been stated, the treatment is chiefly homophonic. Where there is an opportunity for imita-

tion, Palestrina makes use of it but only in passing and without troubling to carry out the imitations in detail. The next section, *"quia hodie,"* begins in pure homophonic style with the so-called "Stabat Mater triads" (as Palestrina uses this chordal progression in a particularly expressive manner at the beginning of his famous *Stabat Mater,* it has come to be designated in this way).

At *"descendit"* a freely treated imitative section begins. The alto introduces the theme; the tenor and soprano follow in *stretto* (in the unison and octave respectively). The bass is silent during this development, but to compensate for silence, it takes the lead in the next section where it is followed by the tenor, soprano, and alto in succession (likewise in *stretto*). These different entrances, however, have in common only the descending skip of the fifth, which is used as a setting for the word *"descendit";* after this skip each voice goes its own way; the soprano, in fact, drops out entirely. As a whole, the character of this section, therefore, is halfway polyphonic. The fourth and next to the last part, on the other hand, is entirely strict and regular. In the theme one will recognize without difficulty the beginning of the Gregorian gradual *Haec dies:*

Haec   di -   -   -   -

A canonic duet between the soprano and alto constitute the introduction. As in the beginning of the first section, the imitation takes place in the fifth, the only difference being that now the alto comes first and the soprano answers. The tenor (with the initial note lengthened) and the bass (in the fifth below) enter after five measures, but with a treatment which differs from that in the upper voices. A final entrance of the theme (in the soprano) closes this section. The next and last episode, finally, comprises one of those wonderful, dance-like portions in dactylic rhythms which Palestrina and his contemporaries at times use to express artless joy. With the exception of a single imitation between the soprano and tenor, the style is entirely homophonic. In bars 71 and 82 on the third half notes one will notice dissonances which seem to be treated contrary to rule. Here, however, a modification of the rhythm takes place, which is not apparent in the notation. Measures 71 to 72 and 82 to 83 really change to the large 3/1 meter, and the dissonances referred to are therefore actually legitimate suspension dissonances:

Such changes from smaller meters to larger are not unusual in ternary rhythm in the fifteenth and sixteenth centuries, and for that matter they can be found even in Händel and Mozart.

Finally, a résumé of the different kinds of styles found in the various sections of the motet gives the following result:

1. (*a*) strict polyphonic, (*b*) strict polyphonic;
2. (*a*) strict polyphonic, (*b*) free polyphonic;
3. (*a*) homophonic, (*b*) free polyphonic;
4. strict polyphonic;
5. homophonic.

This résumé indicates how one style gives way to the other, how provision is constantly made for change and relief so that nothing tires the listener.   Avoided, above all, is the constant, exact imitation, which often produces such a pedantic and trivial effect in Palestrina's Netherland predecessors.

Chapter IX

THE MASS

THE CATHOLIC HIGH MASS consists of five principal musical liturgical parts:
1. *Kyrie eleison.*
2. *Gloria.*
3. *Credo.*
4. *Sanctus-Benedictus.*
5. *Agnus Dei.*

These texts (or songs), which together constitute the *ordinarium missae,* are fixed in the sense that, except for certain services which have remained in an older arrangement, they are used with exactly the same words and in the same sequence in every mass.

The *proprium de tempore,* the other principal group of texts (or songs) in the mass celebrations of the Catholic Church, likewise takes a regular place in the liturgy; every mass and every sung high mass has an *introitus,* a *graduale,* and so on, but the texts or songs which belong to the different forms vary from service to service. The principal portions of the *proprium* are the following:
1. *Introitus* (introductory, before the Kyrie).
2. (*a*) *Graduale,* (*b*) *Alleluia* or *Tractus* (after the Epistle).
3. *Offertorium* (for the taking of the offering).
4. *Communio* (for the communion).

The polyphonic musical forms associated with these texts of the *proprium* are called motets, while the music to the five parts of the *ordinarium* is always designated as the mass whether it is polyphonic or for a single voice.

The complete text of the Catholic mass, that is, the ordinary of the mass, is as follows:

1. *Kyrie eléison, Christe eléison, Kyrie eléison.*

2. *Glória in excélsis Deo. Et in terra pax homínibus bonae voluntátis. Laudámus te. Benedícimus te. Adorámus te. Glorificámus te. Grátias ágimus tibi propter magnam glóriam tuam. Dómine Deus, Rex coeléstis, Deus Pater omnípotens. Dómine Fili unigénite Jesu Christe. Dómine Deus, Agnus Dei, Fílius Patris. Qui tollis peccáta mundi, miserére nobis. Qui tollis peccáta mundi, súscipe deprecatiónem nostram. Qui sedes ad déxteram Patris, miserére nobis. Quóniam tu solus sanctus. Tu solus Dóminus. Tu solus Altíssimus, Jesu Christe. Cum sancto Spíritu, in glória Dei Patris. Amen.*

3. *Credo in unum Deum. Patrem omnipoténtem, factórem coeli et terrae, visibílium ómnium, et invisibílium. Et in unum \Dóminum Jesum Christum, Fílium Dei unigénitum. Et ex Patre natum ante ómnia sáecula. Deum de Deo, lumen de lúmine, Deum verum de Deo vero. Génitum, non factum, consubstantiálem Patri: per quem ómnia facta sunt. Qui propter nos hómines, et propter nostram salútem descéndit de coelis. Et incarnátus est de Spíritu sancto ex Maria Vírgine: Et homo factus est. Crucifíxus étiam pro nobis: sub Póntio Piláto passus, et sepúltus est. Et resurréxit tértia die, secúndum Scriptúras. Et ascéndit in coelum: sedet ad déxteram Patris. Et íterum ventúrus est cum glória, judicáre vivos et mórtuos: cujus regni non erit finis. Et in Spíritum sanctum, Dóminum, et vivificántem: qui ex Patre, Filióque procédit. Qui cum Patre, et Filio simul adorátur, et conglorificátur: qui locútus est per Prophétas. Et unam sanctam cathólicam et apostólicam Ecclésiam. Confíteor unum baptísma in remissiónem peccatórum. Et exspécto resurrectiónem mortuórum. Et vitam ventúri sáeculi. Amen.*

4. *Sanctus, Sanctus, Sanctus, Dóminus Deus Sábaoth. Pleni sunt coeli et terra glória tua. Hosánna in excélsis.—Benedíctus qui venit in nómine Dómini. Hosánna in excélsis.*

5. *Agnus Dei, qui tollis peccáta mundi: miserére nobis. Agnus Dei, qui tollis peccáta mundi: miserére nobis. Agnus Dei, qui tollis peccáta mundi: dona nobis pacem.*

In the music of the fifteenth century the mass is usually treated as a cantus firmus composition; that is, it is constructed on a sacred or secular melody which is placed in the tenor and only rarely exercises a melodic influence on the other voices. But, as imitation gradually comes to be more important in the technique of composition, little by little the cantus firmus mass disappears, and from the second quarter of the sixteenth century on the purely imitative treatment of the mass predominates. To be sure, cantus firmi are often used in this period, but a particular basic melody does not appear exclusively in one voice, though portions of it, at least, appear in all voices. Especially characteristic of the masses of the sixteenth century is a form which might be called "transcription mass"; transcription masses are made of other smaller polyphonic compositions (motets, chansons, madrigals, or songs) in such a way that they transcribe or paraphrase them.[1]

The transcription mass, which might, therefore, in various circumstances be called a motet, madrigal, chanson, or Lied mass, was often based upon an earlier work of the particular composer; and yet often the composition of another master was used as the basis for the musical construction of the mass. Today, when ideas regarding musical property rights are strict, such a procedure might seem irregular; in the sixteenth century it seemed entirely legitimate and proper. Palestrina himself, for example, used for his masses motets and madrigals of l'Heritier, Hilaire Penet, Lupus, Ferabosco, Verdelot, Jean Richafort, Josquin des Prez, and so on. On the other hand, other composers wrote masses on Palestrina's motets and madrigals. A brief examination of Palestrina's four-part mass *Dies sanctificatus*[2] may serve to explain the transcription technique as well as the mass composition of Palestrina's time in general.

This mass is composed on the Palestrina four-part motet of the same name which was cited in the preceding chapter. With the exception of the last five-part Agnus, it is also written in four parts for mixed chorus. In accordance with the usual practice, the first part, the Kyrie, falls into three distinct subdivisions: Kyrie I, Christe, and Kyrie II.

The first Kyrie begins exactly in the same manner as the motet, of which the two-part introductory theme incidentally constitutes the sole thematic material of this first subdivision.

The Christe is constructed on the second theme, which is also in two parts: (*a*) "*Venite gentes,*" (*b*) "*et adorate Dominum.*"

As may be seen, this section likewise varies only slightly from the corresponding episode in the motet (measure 20). The Kyrie II, on the other hand, is more free in relation to the motet. Here the theme is

---

[1] German musicology uses the term "*Parodiemesse*" (parody mass) in this connection, but this term cannot be regarded as particularly appropriate since the psychological and historic-style-critical elements inherent in this technique are based on a relationship other than that of imitation. At any rate, the expression "parody" has a misleading implication, and I therefore prefer the term "transcription mass," but at the same time I should like to emphasize that I use "transcription" in its broad sense as Liszt, for example, used it to apply to his piano compositions based on the songs of Schubert.

[2] An unabridged reproduction of this whole mass is unfortunately impossible because of the space required. Anyone desiring to study it in greater detail will find it in Volume XV of the complete works of Palestrina and in Proske's *Musica divina*, Annus I, Bd. 1. (Translator's note: It may be found also in the edition of Hermann Bäuerle, Breitkopf und Härtel, Leipzig.)

identical with the form in which it is presented in the alto in measures
31 to 34 (*2b*) with the words *"et adorate"*:

While the first, tripartite division of the mass is imitative and polyphonic in character throughout, the next part, the *"Gloria in excelsis,"* be-

---

[3] See pp. 275 ff, where the entire piece is given.

gins with a syllabic, chordal treatment of the introductory theme of the
motet, which is here placed in the soprano: [4]

The bulk of the text in the parts of the mass which have many words,
such as the Gloria and Credo, does not permit the same musical treatment used in the sections, such as the Kyrie, Sanctus, and Agnus Dei,
where the texts are short. If one were to write the "large" parts in imitative style throughout, they would be disproportionately long, and the
texts would no longer be directly comprehensible. Besides, the performance would require more time than could normally be devoted to these

---

[4] In this connection, note that the Gloria and Credo in the Catholic Church are intoned by the
priest (in Gregorian chant), so that the choir enters with *"Et in terra pax hominibus"* and
"Patrem omnipotentem," respectively.

parts in the service.   The Gloria and Credo are, therefore, usually treated
in homophonic style, with imitations intermixed.   These imitations,
however, are nearly all of a slighter and more transient character and of
shorter duration than the imitations in the other portions of the mass.

The Gloria in the Palestrina period is divided into two parts, of which
the second begins with *"Qui tollis."*   While the first section borrows only
themes *1a, 1b, 2a, 3b,* and *4* from the motet, the second section uses all
eight themes of the motet.   The first and last themes here occur in the
same corresponding positions; the other themes appear in another order.

The Credo is divided into three groups in the Palestrina period: *Patrem,
Crucifixus,* and *Et in Spiritum.*   The first part begins with the introductory theme of the motet; the treatment, however, is here completely
different:

---

[5] The fact that in suspension dissonances the note of preparation and the dissonance should sometimes carry separate syllables of the text, must be attributed to textual requirements.

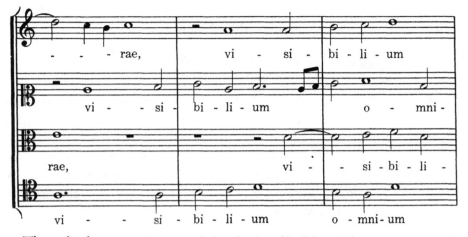

The rule that every return of the theme should use the same text as in the first entrance is here disregarded in favor of a hastening of the textual treatment. The soprano at its entrance continues with the text of the tenor instead of first repeating the words which have just been sung. At *"Descendit de coelis"* the same theme with the descending skip of the fifth is used that appeared in the motet at *"descendit";* the words "descending from heaven" are generally used for tone-painting in the music of Palestrina. The episode *"Et incarnatus est,"* which is accompanied in the liturgy by inclination (bowing of the head or kneeling), is almost always called to special attention in the sixteenth century by broad, solemn chords:

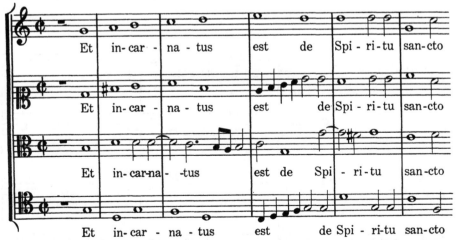

The Crucifixus shows only a slight relation to the motet; of its themes only 2b is actually to be found (at *"cum gloria judicare"*) in the same

form as in the Christe of the mass. At *"ascendit in coelum"* (ascended
into heaven) we find the traditional tone-painting:

et   a - scen - dit   in   coe - lum

Likewise the third part of the Credo, *"Et in Spiritum"* and so on, does
not follow the motet too closely; and yet four themes are used: namely,
2b, 3a, 3b, and 5.

The Sanctus begins with the introductory theme of the motet, but
Palestrina uses an entirely new treatment. The theme is introduced in
the soprano, while the alto brings in a contrapuntal theme which is then
imitated in the tenor and bass:

In addition to the introductory theme, *1b, 3b, 4,* and *2b* are also used in the Sanctus. The Benedictus, which, like the Sanctus, is generally constructed with broad themes and complete imitations, is based exclusively upon *2a* and *3b,* while the following Hosanna depends entirely on *2b.*

The Agnus I begins with the theme *1a* in the soprano, and this is accompanied in the alto with a counterpoint which the tenor imitates and afterwards the soprano takes up while at the same time the bass sings *1a.*

For the rest, this somewhat brief piece is restricted to the use of the themes *1a* and *4.* The five-part Agnus II, which concludes the mass and

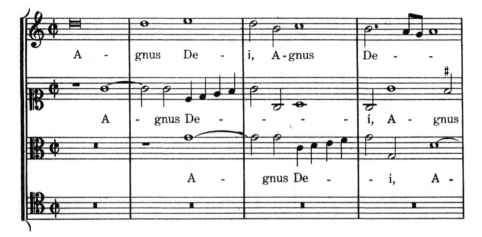

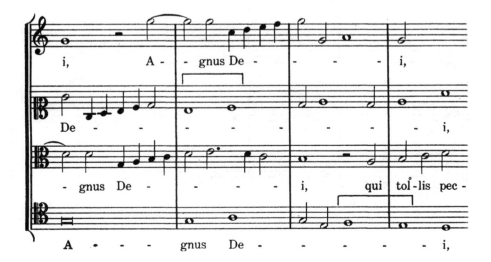

in which the second alto is a canon in the fourth above in relation to the
tenor, begins with the theme *2a* worked out strictly:

After this, theme 3*b* is treated, and the mass closes with a kind of paraphrase on the dactylic episode at the end of the motet.

A comparison between the mass and the work upon which it is based must obviously reveal the richer and more varied technique of the expanded form. The mass in the sixteenth century was generally regarded as the arena for technical skill; here a musician could first of all demonstrate his dexterity, here he was afforded an opportunity to reveal all sides of his ability in composition. The transcription technique which Palestrina uses in the mass just discussed bears a considerable resemblance to the variation technique. The composition here is closely related to the original material upon which it is based; and this is not unlike the relation of the variation to its theme. Moreover, in the mass the free play of artistic fantasy is somewhat restrained by liturgical and practical considerations. Transcription is accordingly the most appropriate term for this type of work.

APPENDIX

APPENDIX

THIS SECTION DEALS with certain forms which, although they did not attain their full development in vocal polyphony, nevertheless grew out of it.

THE VOCAL FUGUE

In the sixteenth century *fuga* (Latin for "flight") meant what we to-day call "canon." Later the term was applied to a form which, although occasionally found in Palestrina's time, did not attain its full development until the time of Bach and Händel in the eighteenth century. This form is imitative but not canonic. It begins with the introduction of the theme in one voice (*dux,* "leader" or "subject") in either the tonic or dominant. Then the theme is "answered" by a second voice (*comes,* "companion" or "answer") by having it begin on the dominant, if the subject begins in the tonic, and vice versa. While the second voice has the theme, the first voice continues with a contrapuntal part. If the fugue is in three, four, or more parts, each voice enters in succession, generally alternating on the tonic and dominant; the voices which have already entered continue with counterpoint as each new voice takes up the theme. When all voices have presented the theme, the first portion of the fugue, which is known as the exposition, is ended. Often a short transition follows (in the instrumental fugue this so-called episode is extended considerably, sometimes introducing motives from the theme), and then the counter-exposition begins. As in the exposition, the theme appears in all voices, but the order of the voices and arrangement of the entrances of subject and answer (*repercussio*) are preferably changed. In the fugues of the sixteenth century, three sets of entries of the subject and answer are usually the maximum; indeed even in the eighteenth century one often finds fugues with three such sets of entries. Bach, to be sure, often exceeds this number or leaves out the transitions between the different sets of entrances, so that it is hard to tell where one section ends and the next begins. In the following exercises we shall restrict ourselves to the normal maximum number of three sets of entrances, which is most appropriate for the length of the fugue. In the third and last group of entries the imitation often takes place in *stretto*. Here, too, the use of ingenious devices such as imitation in contrary motion, by augmentation, or by diminution is suitable and natural. In the section on imitation mention was made (p. 163) of the fact that the composers of the sixteenth century at times used the tonal answer, but that they, as a rule, preferred the real form. Likewise in the matter of the correct answering of the sequence of whole and half tones, and so on, the earlier period was less strict than the later.

If one would remain strictly in the tonality and not introduce any chromatic changes, an exact answer to the theme in imitation in the fifth above or fourth below (as used in the fugue) can be carried out only if the theme begins with the tonic and takes its tonal material from the

so-called tonic hexachord  (C major and A minor,

in A major and F-sharp minor: A-F sharp, etc.), since this hexachord represents the longest series of tones which is repeated exactly within the scale:

Tonic hexachord   Dominant hexachord

Consequently if a theme in C major which begins on the tonic uses a B, for example:

it cannot be imitated exactly without the introduction of a sharp before F, since the answer otherwise would have half-tone steps from the second to the third and from the third to the fourth notes, where the subject has major seconds:

Such a consideration did not, as a rule, trouble the composers of the Palestrina period; in Bach's time such a theme would usually be answered thus:

That is, this theme lies within the dominant hexachord and can logically be answered only in the fifth below or the fourth above:

Since the theme, however, is in C major and the subject begins on the tonic, the answer must necessarily begin on the dominant G, and one therefore replaces the first tone in the correct answer (d) with G, while the other tones remain unchanged. In this way the form (c) is obtained. If the theme, on the other hand, begins on the dominant and introduces an F, for example:

it then falls within the scope of the tonic hexachord and therefore can be correctly imitated in the fifth above or the fourth below:

Since the C is the proper initial tone of the answer, we get the following form:

These rules may be summarized as follows:

1. If a theme begins with the tonic and then goes beyond the tonic hexachord, the answer in the fifth above or fourth below must be lowered a second from the second tone on.

2. If a theme commences on the dominant and exceeds the range of the dominant hexachord, the answer in the fourth above or in the fifth below must be raised a second from the second tone on.

As has been said, these rules did not hold in the sixteenth century, and even in the time of Bach they were occasionally disregarded, especially where a treatment in strict accordance with the rule would so change the theme that it could not be recognized easily. Especially in themes which begin with an octave skip or with tonal repetition, one must guard against changes. The following theme (Ionian):

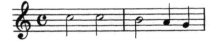

should, strictly speaking, be imitated as follows:

But the character of the theme would thereby be so changed that one would always prefer the following:

Likewise, a Dorian theme such as:

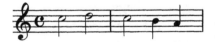

would of course not be answered in this way:

but would be lowered a second after the characteristic octave skip:

In the choice of a fugue theme, the principles emphasized in the section on imitation are of the greatest importance: the theme must be striking, hence rather somewhat angular than too smooth, since angularity helps to make it more recognizable. Moreover the rhythm of the theme as well as that of the counterpoint which accompanies it must not be too uniform and even, or the valuable effect of contrast in the rhythm, which is most desirable between the different voices, is weakened. The theme must always be so introduced that it can be recognized immediately. It is therefore best if it enters after a rest or after a clear-cut melodic section. For example, it would not be good if the first note of the theme should at the same time be the closing tone of the preceding phrase:

Theme

Here one would unquestionably misunderstand the situation and take the F instead of the D as the initial tone of the theme. The entrance is clearest if it comes after a rest; and yet in this case one must take care that the voice concerned drops out before the rest in an appropriate manner. For example, it should not close on a note value less than a half note, and it is best for it to come to an end with some cadential figure. In *stretti* slight rhythmic or melodic changes in the theme may be necessary, but the essential character of the theme must not be impaired in any way. It is, therefore, advisable that in the selection of a fugue theme one first makes sure that the particular theme lends itself to *stretto* treatment. If the answer enters in *stretto* it is, moreover, not limited to the tonic and dominant as initial tones but can also begin on other tones. As in imitation, each voice needs to reproduce only as much of the theme as the preceding voice has sung at the time of its entrance.

Let us now try to write a fugue for two voices. Since it is best for each voice to enter after a rest, the composition must continue at certain places in one part. Such episodes should, nevertheless, be kept as short as possible. Indeed, the transition from the exposition to the counter-exposition must not be too noticeable. A too noticeable transition can be avoided by a chain of small note values. On the other hand, before the *stretto* a stop (often a general pause) is entirely in place:

Exposition

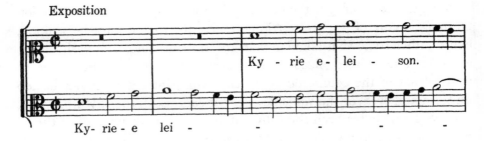

Ky - rie e - lei - son.

Ky- rie - e lei - - - - -

Counter - exposition

Ky - rie e - lei - - -

- - son.

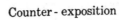

Stretto

_ - - - son. Ky -

Ky - rie e - lei - - son. Ky - rie e -

rie e - lei - - - - - - son.

lei - - - - - - - son.

Exposition

Be - ne - di - ca - - mus. Do -

Be - ne - di - ca

Like three-part imitation, the three-part fugue also requires the most complete chords possible. It is especially important to have the entrance of the third voice produce a complete triad. A most effective entrance is attained if the entering voice makes a suspended dissonance out of a tied note (compare p. 198). If the entrance of the preceding voice is on the tonic, the third voice normally begins on the dominant, and so on; but it sometimes happens—especially when the middle voice has the subject first—that the second and third voices enter on the same tone.

As in the two-part fugue, one must also take care that the transition from the exposition to the counter-exposition is as smooth as possible, though one often sets off the counter-exposition from the *stretto* with the aid of a cadence.   Since a close of the same kind at the end of the second and third sets of entries might easily produce an unvaried, monotonous effect, one often modulates in the second set of entries to a key related to the chief key (compare p. 82) or ends with a half, or deceptive cadence, for example (Aeolian):

The following three-part fugue treats an Ionian theme three times with the last in *stretto;* but there the imitation does not come on the tonic and dominant as usual, but on the second and sixth of the scale.

Exposition

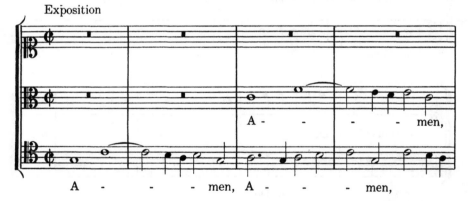

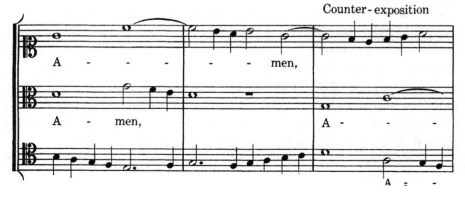

Two examples of four-part fugues are now presented, one in the
Dorian, the other in the Mixolydian mode. The latter fugue is taken
from the mass *Dies sanctificatus* by Palestrina, which has already been
mentioned. It may seem remarkable that this Mixolydian composition

should begin with an Aeolian imitation on A and E and that it brings in the principal mode of the mass only at the end. But this is probably because the theme, which is taken from the motet *Dies sanctificatus* (see p. 244), begins there with A. In the exposition, soprano and tenor each introduce the theme twice in a slightly changed form; moreover, Palestrina uses *stretto* even here. The entrances follow each other very closely only in the third set of entries.

Stretto

Exposition   Palestrina

Stretto

Fugues on two themes are called double fugues; on three themes, triple fugues, and so on. Such forms, however, did not occur in the sixteenth century, but belong exclusively to the time of Bach. To illustrate this type of fugue in brief, a double fugue by J. J. Fux is given below, a composition which is to a certain extent intermediate between the Palestrina style and the eighteenth century. This Dorian fugue is constructed on two themes. After the bass introduces the first theme, the tenor imitates it in the fifth above while the bass, as counterpoint against the tenor, brings in the second theme. This procedure is frequently used in double fugues. And yet one can make use of another form in which each theme is first introduced separately and then both are introduced together. In the fugue before us, both themes wander

in exact succession from the bass on up through all four voices. With
the tenth measure, this wandering of the voices comes to an end and with
it the exposition. Before the upper part has finished singing the second
theme, the tenor begins the counter-exposition in which both themes
occur in all four voices. The third set of entries begins with the tenor
and is treated more freely in that theme I appears only in the tenor and
soprano, while theme II (in somewhat modified form) goes through all
voices (the bass, indeed, sings it twice) and it is treated in *stretto*:

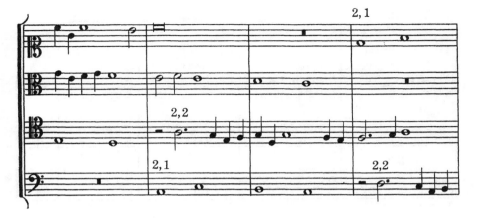

DOUBLE, TRIPLE, AND QUADRUPLE COUNTERPOINT

Double counterpoint means a kind of writing which, without violating the rules of strict counterpoint, provides to the melody a counterpoint that may be used either as an upper or lower part. This technique was known in the polyphony of the sixteenth century, but it first achieved great significance in the instrumental fugue of the eighteenth century.

Double counterpoint in the octave is most frequently used; here one transposes either the upper voice an octave lower or the lower voice an octave higher. By this inversion, it is well known that the prime becomes an octave, the second a seventh, and so on:

$$1 \quad 2 \quad 3 \quad 4 \quad 5 \quad 6 \quad 7 \quad 8$$
$$8 \quad 7 \quad 6 \quad 5 \quad 4 \quad 3 \quad 2 \quad 1$$

As may be seen, all intervals retain their character as consonances or dissonances, with the exception of the fourth, which becomes a fifth, and vice versa. The writing of double counterpoint in the octave offers no difficulties, therefore, and it is done in accordance with the usual rules concerning the treatment of the interval combinations with one exception: that the fifth also is to be regarded as a dissonance. If one wishes to avoid crossing the two voices, the interval between them must not exceed the octave.

An example of double counterpoint in the octave:

A similar example from the Credo of the mass *Iste Confessor* by Palestrina:

If, in double counterpoint in the octave, one avoids all similar motion and all suspended dissonances, one can add to each part a parallel part in the third or tenth above and in this way get a four-part composition:

Outside of counterpoint in the octave, counterpoint in the tenth and twelfth are among the more common forms. The inversion in the tenth changes the intervals as follows:

1   2   3   4   5   6   7   8   9   10
10 9   8   7   6   5   4   3   2   1

Thus all consonances retain their consonant character, just as all dissonances remain dissonant upon inversion. But the perfect consonances become imperfect, the imperfect perfect; parallel thirds and sixths, as well as progressions in similar motion to thirds or sixths, are therefore not usable. In other words, only oblique and contrary motions are possible in these exercises. Dissonant suspensions cannot be used, since correctly treated fourths, sevenths, and seconds must resolve as follows upon inversion: sevenths into octaves, fourths into fifths, and ninths into octaves.

Exercises such as those above may be increased by one part if one adds
either a parallel part in the tenth below to the upper voice or one in the
tenth above to the lower part:

In the inversion in the twelfth the intervals are altered as follows:

1	2	3	4	5	6	7	8	9	10	11	12
12	11	10	9	8	7	6	5	4	3	2	1

The chief point to observe here is that the sixth, upon inversion, becomes a seventh and that, consequently, it must be treated as a dissonance:

If one avoids suspensions and progressions in similar motion, one can make the exercise three- or four-part by adding parallel voices in thirds or tenths over the lower voice or under the upper voice:

Invertible counterpoint in more than two parts is called triple counterpoint if there are three parts, quadruple if there are four parts, and so on. It is necessary for every single voice to move correctly in relation to all the other voices in accordance with the rules given in this book. In this type of counterpoint, when it is in the octave, all fifths must be treated as dissonances, regardless of the voices in which they occur. It must be noted that fourths cannot be covered by placing consonances below them, as in simple counterpoint. The following example illustrates quadruple counterpoint in the octave:

etc.

*   *   *   *   *   *

Through the study of the exercises in this textbook the pupil should now be in a position comparable to that attained in the realm of languages if he has mastered a basic language. For example, one who has made himself thoroughly familiar with the Latin language finds the way open to a noble world literature. Yet more important, he has assimilated not only a single language but such a fundamental knowledge of language in general that it will be easier for him to understand all modern western European languages and their literatures.

It is exactly the same with the Palestrina style, where the chief problems of all musical technique appear clearly and plastically as perhaps in no other style species and where these problems are treated with almost matchless certainty and naturalness. If one could imagine a music which does not subordinate itself to the expressive will of an artistic personality or of a historic epoch but follows only its own purely musical laws and urges, one may ask whether such a music would not come closer to the Palestrina style than to any other.

To present this "pure" music—with the Palestrina style as the medium —is the ultimate aim of this book. At best, the pupil may learn from it something about the inmost nature of music; at worst—although it is to be hoped no one will come off so badly—he may acquire some skill in a kind of musical *pasticcio* through a vain attempt to imitate a great historical style.

The classical style is presented here not to be superficially imitated, but so that its fruitful and eternally valid fundamental principles may be understood.

SUMMARY OF THE MOST IMPORTANT
CONTRAPUNTAL LAWS AND RULES

Melody

Intervals

All augmented and diminished intervals are forbidden (p. 85). The major and minor second and third, perfect fourth, fifth, and octave can be used in both directions; the minor sixth is allowed, but in ascending motion only (p. 85).

Succession of Intervals

In ascending motion it is best for the large intervals to precede the smaller; in descending, for smaller intervals to come first (p. 86). This rule is less strict with the longer note values, but with quarters it is rigid (p. 87). Furthermore, in quarter-note movement the succession of stepwise progressions and skips is restricted to two possibilities: a third followed by a second in ascending motion, a second followed by a third in the opposite direction (pp. 119 f.).

Skips

Skips are to be filled in as much as possible (pp. 85 f.). Skips upward from the accented quarter note are forbidden (p. 87). Two or more skips in the same direction are not allowed in quarter-note progressions (p. 89). Skips of a third downward from an unaccented quarter are always to be compensated by a succeeding step of the second upward (p. 121).

Stepwise Progression

Unaccented quarters approached by step from below must, as a rule, be continued upward by step (p. 120).

Rhythm

Eighth notes may be used only two at a time, must occur in the place of an unaccented quarter, and must be approached and quitted by step (p. 93). Two quarter notes may not occur alone in the place of an accented half in the measure; either a quarter note must precede or follow them, or the first of the two quarters must form part of a suspension, or a suspended half note must follow the second quarter (p. 140). The smallest note value which may be used in a suspension with a note of equal value is the half (p. 141). In the suspension the only place where the smaller note value may precede the greater is in the cadence (p. 141).

CONSONANT COMBINATIONS

Consonances

In chordal combinations one regards as consonances the perfect unison, fifth, octave, twelfth, and so on, which are called perfect consonances, and likewise the major and minor forms of the third, sixth, tenth, and so on, which are called imperfect consonances (p. 98).

Parallel fifths and octaves are forbidden (pp. 98 f.).

Hidden fifths and octaves are forbidden in first, second, and third species in two parts. On the other hand, in fourth species in two parts where they are delayed by suspensions, they are permitted, and they may be used in a similar manner in fifth species in two parts. In free two-part writing they can also be used in other ways—but only with the greatest care (pp. 100 f.). In three-part writing hidden fifths and octaves are permissible between outer and inner voices. Hidden fifths may also occur between outer parts, but in such cases it is best for the upper part to move by step. Hidden octaves, on the other hand, are to be avoided so far as possible between outer parts (p. 176). In four or more parts, hidden octaves can be used between the outer parts, but here too it is best for the upper part to move by step (p. 203).

Accented Fifths and Octaves

These (a) must be used with care in second species (p. 117) and (b) may be tolerated in third species in exceptional cases between two quarters on accents which are in immediate succession; but octaves

of this sort are not so good (p. 126). (c) They are permitted in suspensions (fourth species) and (d) are treated in accordance with the
same rules in fifth species and in free writing.

Parallel Thirds and Sixths

In whole notes, if possible, not more than four parallel thirds and
sixths should occur in succession (p. 112). In half notes one should
not go too far beyond this number, but in quarters one may use them
more freely (p. 158).

The Unison

(a) The unison may occur in two-part first species only in the first and
last measures (p. 112). (b) It may enter in two-part second species (in
addition to the first and last measures) only on the unaccented portion
of the measure, and the skip by which it necessarily enters is to be counter-
balanced so far as possible by stepwise movement in the opposite direction (pp. 116 f.). (c) The unison is forbidden in two-part third species
(apart from the first and last measures) on the first quarter of the measure,
but otherwise may be freely used (pp. 125 f.). (d) It can be used freely
in two-part fourth species (p. 133). (e) It may be used in two-part free
counterpoint, but must be treated with care (p. 160). (f) It can be employed freely in three and more parts between two or more voices, but
only on the first or last tone may all voices occur in unison (p. 176).

The Beginning

(a) There should be a perfect consonance at the beginning in two-part
first, second, and fourth species, but the fifth below the cantus firmus is
forbidden (p. 112). (b) The beginning may occasionally have an imperfect consonance in two-part third species if the counterpoint begins with
an upbeat (p. 125); and (c) it may have the full triad in three or more
parts, but in such cases the third must always be major. If the third enters
as an upbeat it may be minor; here one can begin only with a full or empty
triad, that is, one in which the third is missing (pp. 176 f.).

The Close

(a) The close must always be made with a perfect consonance in two-
part writing; if the counterpoint is in the lower part, only the unison

and octave may be used (p. 112). (b) It may consist of a perfect triad or of a "triad" with fifth or third missing in three and more part writing. The third here must be major (pp. 176 f.).

DISSONANT COMBINATIONS

Dissonances

All augmented and diminished intervals, the perfect fourth, major and minor second, seventh, ninth, and so on, are dissonances (p. 98).

In the First Species

Dissonances cannot be used (p. 111), but in three or more parts, the fourth between an upper and a middle part or between two inner parts may be used as a consonance (p. 175). This rule likewise applies to the remaining species.

In the Second Species

Dissonances may occur, but only as passing notes (p. 116).

In the Third Species

The dissonance can be used as a passing note as well as a lower auxiliary or returning note, but it must always be approached and quitted by step. The sole exception to this rule is the so-called *cambiata,* in which an unaccented dissonant quarter introduced by step from above is quitted by a skip of the third downward followed by a step of the second upward (p. 125).

In the Fourth Species

The dissonance may occur on the accented part of the measure, but in such a case it must be tied over from the preceding unaccented beat (where it must be a consonance), and it must be led stepwise downward to a consonance on the following unaccented beat (p. 131). The sole exception is the so-called consonant fourth, a fourth which is introduced at the place of the unaccented half note over a stationary tone in the bass, to be tied over to the succeeding strong beat and finally to be regularly resolved on the following unaccented beat (pp. 193 f.). If, in two-part writing, the counterpoint is in the upper part, only the perfect fourth and the major or minor seventh can be used as suspension dissonances; if the counterpoint is in the lower part, one can use (in two-part writing) only the major and minor seconds as suspension dissonances. Augmented and diminished intervals cannot be used here (p. 132). In three or more parts, however, other dissonances may be used when they occur simultaneously with "good" suspensions (p. 188).

In the Fifth Species

An unaccented half which comes after a suspension or a whole note can be a dissonance if the dissonance is treated in accordance with the rules for the second species, but cannot be dissonant if preceded by quarters. Likewise quarters can be dissonant if they occur after suspensions or dotted halves (pp. 143 f.). Quarters which are tied over from unaccented halves may be dissonant only rarely. On the other hand, suspended quarters can be dissonant if they occur at the place of an unaccented half note (p. 143). If two quarters descending by step follow an accented half, the first of the two quarters may be dissonant; such irregular dissonances, however, are permitted only in descending motion (pp. 143 f.). Dissonant upper auxiliary notes are permissible in quarters if they precede a half or a whole note (p. 144). The first note of the *cambiata* can be a dotted half, and the third note can then be either a quarter or a half. On the other hand, if the first tone of the *cambiata* is a quarter, the third tone must then necessarily be a quarter. The dissonant tone itself (the second tone of the *cambiata*) may in all cases be only of the duration of a quarter (p. 144). Anticipation dissonances may be used, but only as quarter notes, and if approached by step from above (pp. 148 f.). Eighth notes may be dissonant only if they are correctly handled in accordance with the general rhythmic-melodic laws (p. 148).

In Free Counterpoint

(a) In two-part writing, one quarter can form a dissonance with another quarter (note against note) if the dissonance is correctly treated in each voice. This applies likewise to writing in three or more parts in which all voices move in quarters; but if in three or more parts stationary tones occur in one or more voices while at the same time two or more voices progress in quarters, these more lively voices may form dissonances with each other freely, provided the relation of each voice is correct with respect to the stationary voices (p. 154). (b) The third of four quarters, of which the first is on the strong accent, can be a dissonance if all four quarters occur in stepwise descending motion and if the fourth quarter moves upward by step while the other part forms a correct syncopation dissonance to the motion in quarters (pp. 154 f.).   (c) While the suspension dissonance proceeds to its resolution the other part may simultaneously move to another tone; in such cases "bad" suspensions, such as the ninth in the upper part, are likewise usable, since they can in this case be resolved upon imperfect consonances (p. 156).   (d) In suspension dissonances the other part may move on after the duration of a quarter if only two steps of the second follow the first (accented) quarter in this voice while the suspension is otherwise correctly treated (pp. 156 ff.); (e) dissonances in half notes cannot be used at all if there is quarter-note movement in another voice at the same time (p. 184).

Index

INDEX

A

A Magyar Népzene, 68
Accent, "reminiscent," 96
Accented fifths and octaves, 117, 126
Accented quarters, 87 (*see also* Quarter notes)
Accidentals, use in notation, 117
Adoramus te Christe, 72
Adrian, 35
Aeolian (*see* Modes)
Agnus Dei, 251 ff.
Agricola, Johann Friedrich, 48
Alberti, Leone Battista, 83
Albinoni, 48
Albrechtsberger, x
Alessi, Giovanni d', vii
Alleluia, 251
Answer in the fugue, 266 ff.
Anthologia Sexta Vocalis Liturgica, vii
Antica musica ridotta . . . , L', 19, 29, 158
Anticipation, 94 f., 148 f.
Architas, 9
Aristotle, 9
Aristoxenus, 9
Aron, Pietro, 30
Ars antiqua, ix, xii, 6, 7, 15
Arsis, 116, 193
Ars nova, 15, 234
Arte del contraponto, L', 29
Art of Counterpoint, The, 147
Artusi, 28, 29, 32, 36, 97
Ascending movement, note values in, 138 ff.
Augmented triad, 176
Auxiliary notes, 11, 94, 121, 141 f.
Ave Maria, 84, 101 ff.

B

Bach, Johann Sebastian, 38, 43, 45 f., 48, 50, 85, 148, 163, 265, 267, 277
Bach, Philipp Emanuel, 48
Bäuerle, Hermann, 253
Banchieri, Adriano, 40
Bar lines, not used, 117
Baroque painting, unity in, xii
Baston, 35
Beethoven, 48
Bellermann, 38, 52, 55, 119, 124, 219
Benedictus, 251 ff.
Berardi, Angelo, 32, 34 f., 41, 43, 91 f.
Binchois, 8, 9, 15
Boethius, 9
Bononcini, 43
Busnois, 8, 9, 11, 15

C

Caccia, 234
Cadence:
  dissonance in, 178
  intermediate, viii
  in the "polyphonic" ecclesiastical modes, 82
  leading tone, 71
  plagal, 75
  seventh degree raised in, 71 ff., 110 f.
  suspension of seventh or second in, 133
Cambiata, 15, 32, 40, 88, 121, 125, 144 ff., 223
Cancrizans, 235
Canon, 234 ff., 265
Cantus figuratus, 11
Cantus firmus, 36 f., 107 f.
Cantus planus, 11